Love's language may be talked with these;
To work out choicest sentences
No blossoms can be meeter;
And, such being used in Eastern bowers,
Young maids may wonder if the flowers
Or meanings be the sweeter.
❧ Elizabeth Barrett Browning

TUSSIE~MUSSIES

THE VICTORIAN ART OF EXPRESSING YOURSELF
IN THE LANGUAGE OF FLOWERS

By Geraldine Adamich Laufer

Still Life Photographs by Starr Ockenga
Theme Photographs by Chipp Jamison

A FLOYD YEAROUT BOOK
WORKMAN PUBLISHING, NEW YORK

Dedicated to my Gardening Grandmother
Mary Druzina Adamich
who taught me the flowers in her garden
and whose memory I cherish.

Library of Congress Cataloging-in-Publication Data

Laufer, Geraldine Adamich.
Tussie-Mussies/by Geraldine Adamich Laufer; photographs by Starr Ockenga and Chipp Jamison.
p. cm.
Includes index.
ISBN 1-56305-106-0
[1. Tussie-mussies. 2. Flower language. 3. Tussie-mussies—pictorial works.
I. Title.]
SB449.5.T86L38 1993
745.92'3—dc20   92-50927
CIP
Workman books are available at special discounts when purchased in bulk for premiums and
sales promotions, as well as for fundraising or educational use. Special editions can also be cre-
ated to specification. For details, contact the Special Sales Director at the address below.

Workman Publishing Company, Inc.
708 Broadway
New York, NY 10003

Printed in Hong Kong
First printing November 1993
10 9 8 7 6 5 4 3 2 1

ACKNOWLEDGMENTS

*E*arly research for *Tussie-Mussies* was funded by a generous grant from the Herb Society of America.

Two special mentors made significant contributions to the development of this book, but did not live to see it published: Elisabeth Woodburn, past president of the Antiquarian Booksellers' Association of America, provided sage advice, and Anne Lyon Crammond, former executive director of the Atlanta Botanical Garden, was my enthusiastic advocate. I also wish to thank Floyd Yearout, who lent his great insight and savoir faire during the formative stages.

Tussie-Mussies is a visual book, and I owe tremendous gratitude to both of my photographic collaborators: Chipp Jamison, for his early confidence in my project and for his generosity, patience and flexibility, allowing me to appear in his Atlanta studio whenever some unusual floral combination was in bloom; and Starr Ockenga (who for weeks converted her New York studio into a tussie-mussie salon), for her passion for historical accuracy and for her personal warmth and elegance, which shine through every photograph she contributed. Many contributed to the richness of the imagery: Starr's photographic assistant, Michael McLaughlin, and also friends and suppliers of Victoriana, especially Patricia Barbiero and Ruth Giordano, Dorene Burger and Nancy Marshall, Marlene Harris and Nancy Rosen. Sylvia Weinstock Cakes contributed the exquisite tussie-mussie of sugar dough flowers, and Muffie Michaelson, Katie Leonaitis, Diane Grinnell, Sharon Eubanks, Mary Beth Kelly, Mildred Pinnell and Dean Pailler shared the bounty of their gardens. Phyllis Slaight very generously loaned her beautiful posy holders; James Moretz, Jeri Schwartz and Dorothy Veirs were valuable sources of information on posy holders. Silversmith Susan Wood provided the lovely contemporary posy pin.

My research was enhanced by the work of Beverly Seaton of Ohio State University, and aided by Charlotte Tancin of the Hunt Institute for Botanical Documentation, Susan Guerney and Kathy Meehan of the Smithsonian Institution. In the task of matching antique French and modern Latin plant names, Kathy Aitken, Ron Determann, Mindy McGovern, Katherine Montgomery and Irene Seay contributed welcome help; Dottie Fuqua, Marion Gwinner, Barbara Humphreys, Leah Capes Mazade and Kitsy Mostellar provided books and information. Ty Leslie and Felicia Rickman reviewed my glossary for floral accessibility. Bud Allen, Bob Stein and John Wright shared generously from their experience. Betty Childs gave incisive advice on the first draft.

This book owes much of its vitality and clarity to Peter Workman and to his truly exceptional staff at Workman Publishing. My thanks go especially to my editor, Ruth Sullivan, whose demanding acumen is apparent on every page, and to the meticulous Kathy Ryan. Robbin Gourley and Lisa Sloane designed and assembled a gorgeous layout.

Finally, trusting that "the last shall be made first," I am delighted to be able to thank my family and my dearest husband David for his encouragement, advice and love.

*T*ABLE OF CONTENTS

THE LANGUAGE OF FLOWERS

FLORAL LORE THROUGH THE AGES

VICTORIAN FLORAMANIA

MAKING A TUSSIE-MUSSIE

A Step-by-Step Guide ❧ *54*

SIXTY THEME TUSSIE-MUSSIES

GLOSSARY

*I*t has always been a joy to receive flowers—a sumptuous armful of roses, a trailing bunch of arbutus or honeysuckle, a tiny fistful of wildflowers. But how much greater the pleasure if the flowers themselves carry a meaning. In the Victorian era the diverting Language of Flowers added fascination to the little bouquets lovers exchanged. And the giving and receiving of tussie-mussies became a craze. A tussie-mussie or "talking bouquet" or "word poesy," as it has been called, is a circular nosegay whose fragrant herbs and flowers carry a message in the Language of Flowers—love, condolence, good luck, or a variety of other sentiments.

These entrancing little tussie-mussies have been a part of human experience forever, it seems. The ancients delighted in them; to Aztec warriors they were as indispensable as their weapons; in medieval Europe, people carried tussies as a prophylactic against the plague. Flowers were used in all the ceremonies and rituals of daily life—festivals of the harvest, childbirth, marriage and death; in medicine, in church and in courts of law. From the sixteenth century on, tussie-mussies served as essential accessories and were carried, worn in the hair, pinned to gowns, or suspended from chains. The Victorians turned flower-giving into an art and practiced the floral language with a vengeance—their bouquets could carry such a complex freight of sentiments that dozens of dictionaries were published to help decipher their messages.

To some plants and flowers a persistent meaning has been ascribed over the ages. One of these is rosemary, which from ancient times has been understood to signify remembrance and constancy. Lilies have suggested Purity; ivy, Fidelity; laurel, Victory and roses, Love. In the nineteenth century such meanings were codified and published in popular books that enabled the giver of a bouquet to express himself in the Language of Flowers. Since each flower had a meaning, assembled together, they spelled out a complex thought. In prim Victorian society, the tussie-mussie was a discreet messenger for the daring (but proper) suitor, for the inarticulate but sympathetic friend, or for the polite guest. The Language of Flowers, with its often ingenious "grammar," was a source of much anxious interest and excitement to the lovers who communicated in it. Indeed, it has been called the language of the love affair because most of the meanings ascribed to particular flowers represent the waxing and waning emotions of romantic love.

The idea of tussie-mussies is being revived today. There are old English gardens once again where the delicious herbs and flowers of times past flourish—mignonette, lemon balm, lavender, rosemary, roses. A number of Language of Flowers books are in circulation. For anyone who would like to compose her (or his) own tussie-mussie, we offer a Step-By-Step Guide (page 54). And with the help of the "Vocabulary of Flowers" (page 133), you can spell out meaningful floral messages without ever having to write a word. To delight and inspire you, floral poet Geraldine Laufer has composed sixty tussie-mussies, with both traditional and contemporary wishes. There are bouquets that say Happy Anniversary, wish Good Luck on a Job Interview, express Sympathy, declare Devotion, arrange a Tryst, inspire Creativity, or even challenge a Rival. It gives new meaning to the phrase "Say It With Flowers."

THE LANGUAGE OF FLOWERS

Talking Bouquets

What is a girl to make of this? A messenger has just delivered a box to her father's door, with her name on it. Upon removing the lid in the privacy of her bedroom, she finds a glowing, fragrant bouquet tied up with a neat collar of paper lace and streamers of blue ribbon. The card, which she extracts from its nest between a red rose and a daisy and opens with trembling fingers, tells her what she'd hoped—that the flowers are from Mr. D.L.

Being a modern nineteenth-century miss, however, she doesn't just take a deep, ecstatic sniff and run off to find a posy holder in which to display her trophy. No, she must find out what the nosegay means. She has a well-thumbed copy of one of those flower language dictionaries that every girl in her set treasures and studies with furrowed brow. Now it's just a matter of naming the flowers in her tussie-mussie and looking them up.

The rose, of course, can mean only one thing: Love. (Thank goodness it isn't yellow, which means decrease of love, or even, heaven forbid, infidelity.) The forget-me-nots confirm the message: True Love. What bliss! And the daisies? Innocence—how sweet! But what about the phlox? Agreement. Does this mean he feels the same as she does? It must. And pansies? Thoughts, of course. Pleasant thoughts, no doubt of it. A few nasturtiums mean Patriotism.

The magisterial Oxford English Dictionary defines "tuzzy mussy" as "a bunch or spray of flowers, a nosegay, a garland of flowers." It first appeared in print in 1440: a "tyte tust or tusemose of flowyrs or othyr herbys." The root "tus" suggests a relationship to tussock, while mussie, a rhyme on tussie, refers to the damp moss pressed around the stems to keep them fresh.

How odd, but it's by no means a negative.
Papa and Mama will think better of D.L. for it.
And the ivy leaves, adding the indispensable
note of green, mean Fidelity. What more could
she ask?

Oh, there's a sprig of dark blue gentian. How
pretty! But, horrors, it means "You are unjust."
Can D.L. have mistaken her reticence for indif-
ference? Just wait till she sees him at church in
the morning!

The mildly titillating nature of the floral language was exciting to young girls, who might spend hours deciphering last night's tussie-mussie. And publishers fueled the fad by offering exquisite special editions of the flower dictionaries, hand-colored, gold-stamped, gilt-edged and leather-bound, as well as inexpensive ones the size of a girl's palm.

Tussie-mussies spoke no language when they first came into being centuries ago, but in the last century the diverting Language of Flowers added fascination to the little bouquets lovers exchanged. The Language of Flowers, which occupied so many minds during the Victorian age, was rooted in two rich beds. One was the western tradition of floral symbolism that filtered down from antiquity, with contributions from mythology, religion and medicine, and from the "emblematic" use of flowers in heraldry during the sixteenth century. The second was the Turkish *Selam*, or language of objects, which contributed to the idea of sending encoded mes-

Language of Flowers.

FADING FLOWERS.
Fade, gentle flower!
All thy white leaves close;
Having thorn thy beauty,
'Tis for repose.
Die, gentle flower,
In the silent sun!
So—all pangs are over,
All thy tasks are done!

7

Toward the end of the eighteenth century, intimate knowledge of the *Selam* may have reached France through a strange route: Aimée Dubucq de Rivéry, a cousin and childhood playmate of Napoleon's Empress Josephine, was kidnapped by Barbary pirates in 1784. Given to the Turkish Sultan, she became his Favorite, and eventually the queen mother of the harem. This romantic story was not forgotten. J.J. Grandville's *Les Fleurs Animées* depicts a fantasy of Tulipa, half flower, half woman, captured by pirates, who becomes the favorite of the Sultan Shahabaan.

sages via symbolic objects—in this case, flowers. The *Selam* (meaning "a greeting") was popularized by European travelers to the Near East in the first half of the eighteenth century and seems to have been brought to English attention by the remarkable, eccentric Lady Mary Wortley Montagu, whose husband served as ambassador to the Porte of Constantinople. In her published correspondence, Lady Mary helped inspire the fashion for the romantic Near East and to popularize the concept of a symbolic language.

In a letter to a friend she wrote: "I have got for you, as you desire, a Turkish love-letter, which I have put into a little box, and ordered the captain of the Smyrniote to deliver it to you with this letter." Inside the box were a pearl, cloves (or carnations), a jonquil, paper, a pear and soap. A lump of coal, a rose, a straw mat, cloth, cinnamon, a torch, gold thread, a lock of hair, grapes, silver or gold wire, and peppercorns completed the message. Lady Mary translated it thus: " 'You are the fairest of the young. I have long loved you and you have not known it! Have pity on my passion! I faint every hour! Give me some hope. I am sick with love. May I die, and all my years be yours! May you be pleased and your sorrows mine! Suffer me to be your slave. Your price is not to be found, but my fortune is yours. I burn! my flame consumes me! Don't turn away your face. Crown of my head! I die—come quickly. Send me an answer.'

"You see," continued Lady Mary, "this letter is all in verses, and I can assure you there is as much fancy shown in the choice of them as in the most studied expressions of our letters, there being, I believe, a million of verses designed for this use. There is no color, no flower, no weed, no fruit, herb, pebble, or feather that has not a verse belonging to it; and you may quarrel, reproach, or send letters of passion, friendship, or even news, without ever inking your fingers."

In 1869, John Ingram explained the matter further to his Victorian readers: "The Turkish dialect, being rich in rhymes, presents a multitude of words corresponding in sound with the names of flowers, and the knowledge of this language consists of being acquainted with the proper rhyme. He traced the origin of this floral system to "the idleness of the harem" and "the desire for amusement and variety which the ladies shut up there, without employment and culture, must feel. It answers the purpose of enigmas, the solution of which amuses the Turkish ladies, and is founded on a sort of crambo or *bout rimé*."

The fascination with the Orient and with botany that characterized the later eighteenth century had much to do with the appearance in

Take this first flower of spring
'Tis an emblem of my heart,
And share with this feeling
May we meet never to part.

In Eastern lands they talk in flowers,

And they tell in a garland their loves and cares;

Each blossom that blooms in their garden bowers,

On its leaves a mystic language bears.

—James G. Percival

9

France of a symbolic language corresponding to the Turkish one. Handwritten lists of many objects and their meanings circulated in the years before the Revolution. Since what rhymed in Turkish did not rhyme in French, the original meanings of the *Selam* became increasingly symbolic.

The object language in France assumed another difference. Flowers replaced the variety of objects used in the Turkish system. The growing interest in botany and exotic plants and their prolific use in decoration and personal adornment made this a natural choice. The fact that both Marie Antoinette and Josephine were infatuated with flowers influenced the way the symbolic language evolved.

Early in the 1800s meanings were codified and published in vocabulary books. The earliest of these, Joseph Hammer-Purgstall's *Sur le langage des fleurs* (1809), noted the connections with the *Selam* while Delachénaye's *Abécédaire de flore* (1811) based his simple list of 190 flowers with symbolic meanings on the handwritten lists that circulated in the French court. But the magnum opus among early flower language books appeared in 1819. It was Charlotte de la Tour's *Le langage des fleurs*, in which the pseudonymous author listed plants appropriate to each season, with explanations for how or why each plant obtained its symbolism. She included a simple dictionary, alphabetized by plant names, with 270 corresponding sentiments. This little book was translated into most European languages, including English, and was widely imitated (and plagiarized).

The year 1823 saw the publication of the first flower language book in English: *Flora Domestica or The Portable Flower Garden,* by Elizabeth Kent. The same year the Germans weighed in with *Selam oder die Sprache der Blumen* by Johann Symanski; it listed 700 flowers by their binomial and common German names, with a rhyming verse in the best *Selam* tradition.

In London, Dr. Henry Phillips published *Flora Historica* in 1824 and, buoyed by its success, *Floral Emblems* in 1825. They contributed historical antecedents to the Language of Flowers and made the connection of the language with tussie-mussies explicit by giving grammatical rules for their presentation. In the United States, Mrs. Elizabeth Gambel Wirt offered *Flora's Dictionary* with original meanings of her own devising.

Language of Flowers books now flooded the market, each volume built directly on its predecessors. Often it was difficult to know who wrote

11

ŒILLET.

BUGLOSE.

VIOLETTE BLANCHE.

CESSE ODORANTE.

them. The author's name might be omitted. Or, if the author was a female, she might prefer to be identified only as "A Lady" or by her initials. By 1857, Sarah Josepha Hale's *Flora's Interpreter*, first published in 1832, had sold over 40,000 copies, not including pirated editions, and could be bought by mail for $2.25 from the ever enterprising *Godey's Lady's Book*. It has been reckoned that fifty-seven writers produced ninety-eight books on the Language of Flowers, in 227 editions between 1800 and 1937.

The design of flower language books varied considerably, from lavishly illustrated colored plates to simple line engravings. All, however, had one thing in common: the vocabulary list of flowers paired with their symbolic meanings. These appeared under such rubrics as "Dictionary for Translating a Bouquet," "Flora's Dictionary" and "Vocabulary List, Part the First." Flowers were sometimes arranged by season of bloom, more often alphabetically by their common names—often regional or colloquial. A few of the larger books with scholarly pretensions supplied the scientific Latin binomial names, an invaluable aid to the modern reader sorting through the unfamiliar and often obsolete plant names.

The lists were sometimes beautifully illustrated, with illuminated initials or typographic decorations, and hand-colored plates that showed sample bouquets with their meanings explained in captions. Unfortunately, their charm has led to the destruction of many books by latter-day print sellers. The 1855 edition of Mrs. Wirt's *Flora's Dictionary* has deep, decorative borders ornamenting the pages of its vocabulary, while James Glass Bertram's *The Language of Flowers: An Alphabet of Floral Emblems* is strictly business, despite its beautiful cover. Small enough to hold in one's palm, the vocabulary list had 609 entries.

Some of the flower language books, like Dr. Henry Phillips' *Floral Emblems*, contained beautiful, hand-colored intaglio illustrations and colored leaves. In one speaking bouquet from *Floral Emblems*, the rose spells Beauty; the foxglove, Youth; and the honeysuckle, Bonds of Love. A message that any anxious lover would welcome.

There are several explanations for the extraordinary popularity of the Language of Flowers during the nineteenth century. Its study was perceived as a genteel occupation of aristocracy and royalty. And Victorian mores held the wearing of flowers to be more suitable for young women than jewelry, so the fashion of carrying hand-bouquets flourished. It was the custom among all classes to give and receive bouquets—and if one wanted them to carry a private message through the Language of Flowers, so much the better. It was customary for men to give their sweethearts bouquets; women and children exchanged them, too. "There are few little presents

Floral Emblems

Declaration of Love.
From Humility to Amiability
Published by Saunders & Otley, 50 Conduit St 1825

FLORAL EMBLEMS
BY HENRY PHILLIPS F.R.S

London Pub.d by Saunders & Otley 50 Conduit Str.t 1825

The Language of Flowers books often included poems mentioning individual flowers by name to accompany each entry. Wordsworth's "Daffodils" was a favorite. Poems focusing on emotions were also suitable. Thus "A Dead Rose" by Elizabeth Barrett Browning might accompany Asphodel, meaning Remembrance of Things Past. An editor wrote in 1839: "In the manual now offered to the public, an attempt has been made . . . to adorn this part of the work with such quotations from the best poets in our language, both native and foreign, as have a direct reference either to the peculiarities of the flowers, or to the sentiments which they are made to express."

more pleasing to a Lady, than a bouquet of flowers; and, if the donor be disposed to give them a greater significance, it will be easy, with this manual before him, to make his selection in such a way as to stamp intelligence and expression on a simple posy," Elizabeth Wirt declared in 1829. Moreover, the Language of Flowers suited the cautious, restrained approach to courtship common in the Victorian era. Since it was considered impolite to overwhelm a lady with passionate terms of endearment, the once-removed declarations made by roses, carnations and other flowers were commendably discreet.

The flower language promoted the keen interest in botany shared by many women in the nineteenth century. Flowers had to be identified before they could yield their meanings. This lent legitimacy to what might otherwise be considered a frivolous pastime. Some authors even recommended that their readers keep their vocabularies well polished by using dried specimens from the herbarium during the winter. Glossaries of botanical terms, botany lessons in the structure of flowers, and Carl Linnaeus' system of classification all appeared in various flower language books as a nod to the scientific aspect of florigraphy. Linnaeus' metaphorical "loves of the plants" led to a conflation of science and romance in suggestible minds.

APPLE BLOSSOM.

Fair pledges of a fruitful tree,
Why do ye fall so fast?
Your date is not so past;
But you may stay yet here awhile
To blush and gently smile,
And go at last.

THE ROSE.—Beauty.

Moore rapturously sings of the Rose:—
Rose! thou art the sweetest flower,
that ever drank the amber shower;
Rose! thou art the fondest child
of dimpled Spring,
the wood-nymph wild!

Finally, the Language of Flowers contains all the elements present in the vastly popular Romantic Movement, whose time frame corresponds to the time of publication of the first, most widely emulated flower language books. Symbolic flowers were included as a matter of course in paintings by the Pre-Raphaelites. And much Romantic poetry used nature to express individual experience and emotion. The Language of Flowers provided an accessible formula for the common man (or woman) to indulge romantic impulses. While not everyone could write enduring Romantic poetry, almost any suitor could tie a tussie-mussie of romantically intended sentiments.

The flower language was comprehensive, including wildflowers, trees, shrubs, vines, herbs, spices, leaves, fruits, vegetables and grains. Fruits, foliage and other plant parts sometimes had meanings of their own. (While orange blossoms signified Bridal Purity, for instance, oranges meant Fertility—a tricky business in which careless errors might prove embarrassing.) Cinnamon meant My fortune is yours; potatoes meant Benevolence; cabbage, Profit. Pineapple symbolized Hospitality; mushrooms, Suspicion; truffles, Surprise. Some of the

In some of the books, the flowers seem to be carrying on a conversation:

Do you love me?
..........................*a coxcomb*

I love you...........*a red rose*

I share your sentiments
.......................*garden daisy*

You may hope
....................*meadow daisy*

Marry me
................*American linden*

more comprehensive lists even had a place for such unlikely candidates as slime fungus (*Tremella nestoc*), meaning Resistance; seaweed (*Agar agar*), Long Life; and moss, Maternal Love.

As the century wore on, the number of flowers included in the vocabularies increased. Meanings far from the traditional centuries-old symbols were added as editors felt free to invent their own. To bowdlerize passages deemed indelicate or indecent was judged a duty by Victorian editors, who took pains to replace too explicitly suggestive sentiments with more guarded ones. "In this symbolic assemblage," wrote one editor in 1825, "the author has carefully avoided all indelicate allusions or double entendres that could be offensive to modesty; his object has been to establish a settled collection of floral emblems, and to render them as amusing as the decorative dress of the poet and the sparkling garb of the wit would allow." For example, in Charlotte de la Tour's book, the meaning for iris is given as Flamme (flame, passion, love); the English Dr. Phillips tamely defines it as Eloquence.

The vocabularies are quaint, naming gentle sentiments possibly unfamiliar to lovers today. The old books show signs of having been well used, with pressed flowers marking certain pages and notations in a fine hand indicating the special importance of one entry or another

❧ *In the language of flowers, red tulips symbolize the declaration of love.*

in long-forgotten lives. In some books, blank colored pages were included for pressing flowers and leaves.

Since these books were intended for actual practitioners of the language, each had a second vocabulary list where sentiments were arranged alphabetically. Readers could look up the emotions they wished to express in this "Index of Interpretations," which would name the appropriate flower. On this basis they (or their florist) composed a bouquet. If more than one flower meant the same thing, all were listed. If a particular flower was not in bloom, there were enough synonyms to make the language more or less functional no matter the season.

Many books provided written and illustrated examples of "talking bouquets." In *Poetry of the Flowers*, Mrs. C. M. Kirtland gives as Example XIII, "Let the bonds of marriage unite us," with this explanation: "1. Bonds . . . Blue Convolvulus; 2. Marriage . . . Ivy; 3. Unite us . . . a few whole Straws."

Meaner sentiments sometimes required expression, as demonstrated in Kirtland's Example XXI: "You are fickle, indiscreet, and affected. Therefore you

Flower symbols were well adapted to Valentine's Day cards. Here, pansies representing "thoughts" proclaim the loving wishes sent to a sweetheart. The card is further embellished with indented zig-zags of the revolutionary new material, celluloid.

WITH LOVING WISHES.
Pansies grow for thoughts,—
Here are some for you,
Just to let you know
Of my affection, true.

are hated." An unusual bouquet was called for: "1. Fickle . . . Abatina; 2. Indiscreet . . . Almond blossom; 3. Affected . . . Cockscomb; 4. Hated . . . Basil."

An intentionally amusing example occurs in *Les fleurs animées* of 1847: "Wormwood has no crown imperial over bittersweet myrtle. You know I have a serpent cactus of whortleberry. Musk plant upside down! Liverwort, we are cistus. Banish all marigolds, and pansy only of the sweet sultan of our pimpernel. Myrtle as high as the heart, and myrtle as high as the eyes forever." Translated, this effusion reads: "Absence has no power over true love. You know I have a horror of treachery. No weakness! Confidence, we are secure. Banish all griefs, and think only of the happiness of our meeting. I love you, and shall love you forever."

Many books featured a Dial of Flowers, or Floral Clock, whose purpose was to provide a way of telling time according to the time of day certain flowers open or close. It may have been inspired by Linnaeus' garden of herbs and flowers, where plants marked the passing of hours by the reliable opening and shutting of their flowers. Four o'clocks, or marvel of Peru, are the most obvious example.

The Calendar of Flowers assigned a specific flower to each day of the year, sometimes noting the saints' days too. A reader could look up

The flower language included trees and their fruits. For example, the oak leaf symbolized Strength, while the acorn meant a Germinal Idea. Philip of Macedonia, the father of Alexander the Great, wore a gold wreath made up of botanically accurate leaves and acorns of the oak (the tree sacred to Zeus). It was found not long ago, intact, within a gold chest in his tomb in Greece.

her birthday or anniversary, or the day she met her current beau, find the flower and infer from its meaning some pleasingly delicate sentiment.

Books sometimes included games to play with real flowers, or decks of flower cards for play during winter months. Often these little games were a sort of key to destiny or a fortune-telling amusement. "Fortuna Flora" guaranteed to "ascertain the particular flowers that best designate your condition, character, and probable success in life."

Where did the meanings for individual flowers originate? While there was no single method of pairing plants and meanings, there seem to have been three sources for the definitions: natural appearance or character, cultural meanings, and meanings arbitrarily assigned by early authors and editors of flower vocabularies and then faithfully followed by others.

The most obvious of these was the first—physical characteristics providing an analogy with some human trait. Thus Strength of an oak, the Promise of a bud, the Fecundity of the many-seeded pomegranate, and so on, are globally recognized symbols.

Legends, folk tales and myths were another rich source of plant symbolism. In

The nineteenth-century craze for the Language of Flowers found many ingenious applications. Among these were decks of flower-language playing cards. Adolescent girls were an obvious market. In "Flower Game," blind-folded players chose a flower from a bouquet to "typify the future consort's character."

This set counts 5
Blue Flowers

4
B

1

Message

Simplicity

FLEUR-DE-LIS
Closed Gentian
Downy Gentian
Fringed Gentian

REEPER
YSUCKLE
ILY

The myth of Daphne and Apollo was the basis for the symbolic meaning of two plants. According to the legend, the independent young huntress Daphne vowed to spend her life as a virgin. When she was pursued by the enamored god Apollo, she screamed out to her father, the river-god, who saved her by turning her into a laurel tree. Apollo watched the transformation with grief and dismay, but vowed that "you shall be my tree. With your leaves my victors shall wreathe their brows." Thus Daphne came to stand for Immortality and the laurel for Victory.

classical Greek mythology, narcissus stood for Egotism, daphne for Immortality, and laurel for Victory and Glory. The second-century work of Artemidorus describes a detailed system of plant symbolism used in dream interpretation. Biblical tradition made the olive branch a symbol of Peace; the palm, of Triumph; and clover, of the Trinity. Ceremonial flowers assumed the symbolism of the ritual with which they were associated: so wedding orange blossoms indicated Bridal Virginity, and St. John's wort, gathered on that saint's eve, promised Protection from Evil. Plants used for healing became associated with their cures. Achillea, or woundwort, cured heartache and became a lover's herb. Comfrey or allheal came to symbolize Comfort, and gillyflowers represented Mirth.

Renaissance sources provided other meanings. Thus pinks signified Divine Love when they appeared with the Virgin Mary, but meant Betrothal when a woman sat for her portrait holding the flower between thumb and forefinger. Heraldry contributed its floral emblems, and historical anecdotes offered certain special meanings. Because Napoleon in exile on Elba promised his followers that he would "return in the spring, with the violets," those flowers came to represent the hopes for his restoration. Disraeli's favorite flower, the primrose, gave its name to the Tory party's Primrose League.

Poetry and literature provided other

sources. In a story by Madame de Staël, the geranium denoted Folly; in another by Rousseau, the periwinkle stood for Happy Memories. Both these meanings found their way into the Language of Flowers.

The lyric poetry of the Elizabethan Age made extensive use of plants and flowers whose connotations added resonance and meaning to the verses. William Hunnis' "A Nosegaye Always Sweete for Lovers to Send" was known to most people who could read, but Shakespeare used this symbolism as naturally as a living creature breathes. The flowers Ophelia distributed each had a meaning that the Elizabethan audience recognized: "There's rosemary, that's for remembrance; pray you, love, remember. And there is pansies, that's for thoughts. . . . There's fennel for you [flattery], and columbines [folly]. There's rue for you [contrition]; and here's some for me. . . . O, you must wear your rue with a difference. There's a

❧ Mother and daughter gilt posy holders.

The garland worn by the drowned Ophelia had significance instantly grasped by Elizabethan audiences: crowflowers for a Fair Maid, nettles suggesting Stung to the Quick, daisies not Wanton, as other sources would have it, but meaning Youthful Bloom, and long purples, suggesting the Cold Hand of Death.

When Charles de Sainte-Maure, later duc de Montausier, was engaged to Julie-Lucine d'Angennes de Rambouillet in 1641, he followed the custom of the age by sending his fiancée a daily bouquet of flowers before the wedding. He went beyond custom, however, in ordering a "garland" of flower paintings and poems, created by the best painters and poets in France. It was a superb folio volume with pages of vellum and a magnificent binding that the bride—suitably astonished and overwhelmed—discovered on her dressing table on her wedding day. *La Guirlande de Julie* was the most sumptuous of all forerunners of the nineteenth-century Language of Flowers. Below, one of the few extant copies of *La Guirlande de Julie.*

daisy [innocence]. I would give you some violets [blue ones, loyalty; white, innocence], but they wither'd when my father died." A significant plant allowed the poet to imply feelings without belaboring the point. Bitter wormwood, willow and yew for Grief, roses for Love, Grace and Beauty, poppy for Oblivion—these and more than 200 other plants, with their familiar meanings, are represented in Shakespeare's plays and sonnets. The nineteenth-century flower language depended on them heavily.

Color added further clarification to the Language of Flowers. White flowers represented spotless Purity and Innocence; red ones, Passion and Ardor. However, there were troublesome contradictions. According to its color, a single type of flower might have various meanings. A pink rosebud, for example, often meant Grace and Beauty; a white rosebud, A Heart Untouched by Love; red, I Love You; and yellow, Friendship. But a full-blown yellow rose stood for Diminution of Love, a yellow tulip for Hopeless Love, a yellow chrysanthemum for Slighted Love. A striped carnation meant Refusal; a yellow one, Disdain; a red one, the Blood of Christ. One could not be too careful.

A plant's scent as well as its native habitat could also contribute to its symbolism. Mint was Refreshing, while the gardenia suggested Transport of Ecstasy. Edelweiss, growing high

LA IONQUILLE.

MADRIGAL.

Dans la Fable, ni dans l'Histoire
Il ne se parle point de moy;
Je ne me puis vanter de posséder la gloire
De descendre du sang ni d'vn dieu ni d'vn roy :
Mais la passion véritable
Que vous témoigne ma couleur ,
Plus qu'vne plus illustre fleur
Me doit rendre recommandable.
O beauté qu'on doit adorer !
Permettez-moy de vous parer,
Et ie m'estimeray cent fois plus glorieuse
Que celle dont l'histoire est cent fois plus fameuse.

De M. le marquis de Montausier.

Jonquilles.

in the Alps, became a symbol for Daring. Oregano, from the dry Mediterranean hills, came to be Joy of the Mountains. Once flourishing at Delphi, where the Oracle dwelt, boxwood came to mean Stoicism and Incorruptibility—virtues associated with the priesthood.

How plants were used dictated meanings as well. Hazel, from which rods to divine water were cut, symbolized Knowledge and Reconciliation. One of rosemary's many meanings, Your Presence Refreshes Me, derived from its use in Hungary Water; its ancient meaning of Remembrance may have come from the fact that it was packed around the dead awaiting burial. Broom, for sweeping, derived its name and meaning, Humility, from its practical use.

Actually making use of the Language of Flowers was another matter. The system of symbols was simple enough, but it was no easy task to convey clear, unambiguous messages. "The evocation of ideas and emotions," wrote one editor, "requires not only an adequate transmitter, but also a receiver sensitive to the message transmitted." Although the notion that flowers represented sentiments was pretty commonly accepted during the nineteenth century, and used metaphorically in the visual and literary arts of the time, it was still possible to miss the

The most imaginative and fantastical of nineteenth-century flower illustrations were done by the French caricaturist J. J. Grandville. Best known for his anthropomorphic illustrations of Fontaine's fables, Grandville used a similar technique to telling effect in his *Fleurs Animées* (1846). Here the witty blending of human and plant features gives each flower a personality and delightful animation. Even his letters do a kind of *danse macabre* with bugs, beetles and butterflies.

Where a girl wore a tussie-mussie presented by an admirer signified her feelings toward him. If she pinned it in her hair he was unlikely to rejoice, for this meant Caution. In the cleavage of the bosom was a little more encouraging, but not very: this signified Remembrance or Friendship. However, if he spied his tussie-mussie placed over her heart he could celebrate, for this was an unambiguous declaration of Love.

significance of a floral communication.

One problem was that to understand the message the recipient must recognize the flower. Common names for flowers varied by region, and even if one knew that name its significance could be misconstrued if the sender knew it by another colloquial name. Since flower language books passed back and forth across the English Channel and the Atlantic, confusion could proliferate. The same flower often had several common names (the buttercup, for example, was also called butterchurn, butter-daisy, fairies' basin, teacup, cuckoo bud and yellow creams), or one name, such as gillyflower, might apply to several different flowers.

The rules for presentation of flowers were a further consideration, for that, too, could determine their meaning. The intent of a bouquet presented upside down was pretty obvious. But the rules got more subtle. Inclining a flower to the right or to the left signified "I" or "thou." You had to consider the hand in which the flowers were presented and even knots in the ribbon could alter the sentiment. Such nuances were easy to overlook.

Without a clear grammar, some argue, the Language of Flowers was hard to understand. Luckily, the demands put upon the language were slight, and a handwritten list of flowers and the sentiments they were to convey provided an easily understood message.

Did anyone ever really use the Language of Flowers? Evidence that tussie-mussies were carried abounds in nineteenth-century fashion plates and florists' periodicals, and the many surviving posy holders are further testimony to their popularity. With so many flower language dictionaries in circulation, it is only plausible that men and women used flowers as a vehicle to carry on their flirtations and romances. Because of the secret nature of the messages, however, actual documentation is rare. Ironically, the strongest proof of the use of a flower language is found in the considerable number of satires directed by less sentimental nineteenth-century writers toward the Language of Flowers.

"The best hypothesis about the Language of Flowers," writes Beverly Seaton, "is that it is a language concocted to amuse women, but the supposed intention is for it to be used by men to speak of love to women . . . in traditional courting procedure." It was probably the rare beau who went to the trouble of working out more than a sketchy message in the Language of Flowers, and many a miss probably read a bit more into her floral text than had been intended.

The
NOSEGAY

25

FLORAL LORE THROUGH THE AGES

The Origins of Tussie-Mussies

The bones of a prehistoric man were discovered a few years ago in the Middle East, ceremoniously laid out and covered with what had been once, 50,000 years ago, a mantle of wild flowers. The pollen grains that remained indicated just which ones were included: yarrow, grape hyacinth, hollyhock, groundsel, woody horsetail. "No accident of nature could have deposited such remains," said the paleobotanist present at the dig. "Someone in the last Ice Age must have ranged the mountainside in the mournful task of collecting flowers for the dead." We can only guess whether they were a comment on the evanescence of life, a tribute to the world's fragile beauty, medicine to be used in a future life, or gifts to appease the gods of the underworld.

In life here on earth, flowers and plants offered food, medicine and adornment. Hallucinogenic plants brought dreams and visions; they were surely sent by the gods, and in thanking and supplicating these gods, men offered fruits and flowers. They have never stopped doing so.

The anthropomorphic deities of the Bronze Age each had their emblematic flowers, and as civilizations developed, flowers acquired more specific and important significance. The Egyptians worshiped leeks and onions, lotus, papyrus and palm, and in time these plants

When they weren't busy sacrificing prisoners of war on the altar of the sun, Aztec noblemen carried tussie-mussies to symbolize their high rank. "No noble ever went on the streets of the city or made a call on a person held in respect without carrying a bunch of flowers. A magnolia of exceeding beauty and fragrance was almost as necessary to an Aztec's dress as the two swords of the Japanese samurai," wrote the editor of *De la Cruz-Badiano Aztec Herbal*.

acquired the status of gods. Ritual offerings—papyrus, poppy, lotus and mandrake—were symbols of death and rebirth along the Nile.

People tucked flowers in their plaited hair, wove them into headbands and chaplets, or sometimes wore a single flower on the forehead. They secured flowers in armbands or placed them in small containers, decorated with lotus, rose and acanthus leaf designs, strapped to the upper arm. Women carried bouquets, sprigs of henna or large single flowers. Both sexes wore circular collars of flowers, leaves, fruits, and blue faïence beads strung together and backed with papyrus. Flower collars also decorated the bodies of the dead. They seemed to remain fresh forever, their colors still bright when the tombs were opened by archaeologists nearly 4,000 years later.

Throughout the Middle East, perfumes and incenses made from flowers, spices and resins were believed to be of divine origin, and the rising fumes acted as a vehicle to carry the soul heavenward.

Death, like happier occasions, called for flowers. They were banked around the funeral couch in the atrium, while branches of pine or cypress were laid at the door of the afflicted house. During the festival of violets in March, and roses in

Athenian vase painting, which tells so much about the social life of the ancient Greeks, shows lithe youths and girls wearing garlands around their necks, wreaths on their heads, and in their hands, flowers, among them roses, violets, hawthorn blossoms and lilies. Priests wore floral crowns, and the altars of the gods were adorned with flowers. Athletes were decorated with flowers in their games, soldiers after victories, and philosophers as they drank wine and argued about virtue. Fresh oak leaves, sacred plant of Zeus, were the chosen foliage for victorious generals; laurel, sacred to Apollo, honored poets and emperors. Aphrodite was crowned with roses, Athena with silvery olive leaves.

The ancient Greeks and Romans carried flowers to ward off disease, believing that their fragrance could both prevent and cure. Apothecaries prescribed aromatic herbs to be sniffed in a time of plague. The Greek physician Diocorides urged the Roman troops in his care to use rue, rosemary and oil of lavender as prophylactics against disease—a practice that survives today.

May, the bereaved laid these flowers on the graves of the dead.

The innumerable festivals of Greece and Rome teemed with flowers. Floralia, an ancestor of May Day, honored the deity Chloris or Flora, patroness of fertility and flowers. At threshing time, in August, Demeter's effigy was adorned with sheaves of wheat and poppies, while a heavily pregnant matron representing the goddess carried an overflowing cornucopia.

Flowers were so integral a part of life's ceremonies that garland-making became an esteemed occupation, with professional garland-makers serving Athena or Minerva, the patroness of craftsmen. So important was this fine art that the name of the best garland-maker has come down to us: Glycena.

Christianity could do little to suppress or alter the impulse to mark significant events with flowers. When a girl was old enough to marry, she wore flowers and ribbons twined in her hair: angelica for Protection, catnip for Beauty, sweet peas and lavender for Chastity, a crown of daisies to indicate she had someone particular in mind. A sprig of basil tucked behind a young man's ear meant that he was courting; a pot of it on the windowsill was a

sign that a daughter of the house was engaged.

Medieval weddings, then as now, called for lavish floral displays. Most important was the bride's crown of flowers, which, with wedding ring and brooch, was a symbol marking the transition from bride to wife. Chaucer describes the bride being prepared for her wedding by her ladies, who combed her hair and crowned her with flowers—roses, lilies, honeysuckle, iris, and above all rosemary, that ancient symbol of loving remembrance. Rosemary has played a more persistent part in marriage ceremonies than any other plant: carried by the bride, strewn in her path, worn by the grooms-men, and floated in the knitting cup.

Nine months later a successful childbirth was ensured by herbs hung over doors and windows and tied in bunches to the bed, among them hazel, hawthorn, garlic, orpine and the powerful rowan. The baby's cradle was never made of any wood that fairy folk favored, such as willow or elder, lest they come in the night and substitute a changeling.

The Celts celebrated May Day, or Belthane, by crowning a May Queen with posies and raising a Maypole, symbol of the tree of life. Around it the merrymakers danced, interweaving ribbons, flowers, and leaves—among them hawthorn, oak and ivy leaves, cinquefoil and

The most famous garland-maker in ancient Greece was Glycena, a devoteé of Athena. Her work was both decorative and prophylactic. She might make a wreath to soothe a headache, or weave a garland of flowers to delight or to inflame passion in a hitherto unfeeling breast.

buttercup. The May King (also known as May Lord, Green Man, Jack-in-the-Green, Robin Goodfellow or Robin Hood) was crowned with leaves. Unable to stamp out this pagan festival, the church Christianized it by simply changing names: the May Queen became the Virgin Mary, Queen of Heaven.

Cypress and yew marked medieval funeral ceremonies, and as badges of grief mourners carried harebell, marigold, aloes, weeping willow and bay. Emblems of remembrance included rosemary, greenbriar, sweet William, forget-me-not and mullein. To protect themselves from the unsettled spirits of the dead, mourners might choose violets, rowan and rue, while to combat the odor of death they carried aromatic herbs in bunches and strewed them on the ground.

Civil and state occasions required their tributes of flowers, too. Visiting dignitaries received bouquets of aromatic herbs and flowers, along with the keys to the city, while the streets were decked with box, ivy and myrtle for royal weddings, baptisms, coronations or state visits. Guilds seeking favors gave the Lord Mayor of London tussie-mussies along with more valuable gifts. Judges, stately in their robes and wigs, carried them into their law courts.

As the altars of ancient Greece and Rome had been festooned with flowers, so the Church in medieval Europe brought flowers to its ceremonies. On holy days the Virgin and the patron

Rosemary, the most versatile of herbs, has long been associated with Love and Remembrance. For millennia the plant has been carried by brides, worn by groomsmen, and used in religious and state processions. When Anne of Cleves married Henry VIII, she wore a crown of fresh rosemary. Whether or not she owed her good fortune to the herb, she was luckier than some of Henry's other wives. He provided her with a handsome income after the divorce.

saint of each parish were crowned with blooms, and nosegays were tucked into their stone hands. The clergy decked themselves with flowers—in part, perhaps, to disguise the unseemly odors of garlic, wine and sweat. As pagan festivals were Christianized, so each plant and flower was given a Christian identity. Saints were assigned whatever flower happened to be blooming on their feast days. Thus Saint George, in April, was given the harebell; Saint Michael the Archangel, in September, the aster. The rose, once sacred to the great goddesses of sexual love and fertility, became the emblem of the Queen of Heaven. Rosemary, which to the Romans represented virginity, became a symbol of purity, fidelity and womanly virtue in the early Christian church. The lily, an ancient mark of both fertility and purity, was appropriated to symbolize the Virgin Birth, and so *Lilium candidum* came to be called the Madonna lily. Medieval paintings of the Annunciation show this elegant plant springing from a flower pot near the kneeling Virgin, just as paintings of other sacred events incorporated flowers to symbolize a host of other virtues, whether humility, grace, or purity.

Finally, bouquets of flowers were essential to daily life, not so much for ornament as for their medicinal value and sweet smells that could mask unpleasant ones, of which there

❧ This medieval knight presents his lady love with newly-plucked double white roses, and she fashions them into a generous tussie-mussie.

were plenty in a world that thought fresh air dangerous. For until very recently, a miasma of foul odors was a ruefully accepted part of civilized life. Nothing would astonish and shock us so greatly, could we be transported back a few centuries to Versailles, Nonesuch Palace, or the streets of any fine city, as the inescapable stench arising from every nook and cranny. Bathing was infrequent, plumbing nonexistent, clothing seldom washable, and animals intimate acquaintances. So it is no wonder that flowers and herbs, perfumes and pomanders were used by men and women to mask what could not be abolished.

It was early in the Middle Ages that "tuzzy-muzzys"—neat little bunches of herbs and flowers—began to be carried everywhere. Their fragrance acted, so people thought, as a prophylactic against contagious disease; it certainly provided a refuge for the nose when the wind blew the wrong way. Held in a warm hand, a herbal bouquet released agreeable odors. Flowers were folded into handkerchiefs or hung round the neck to be sniffed at one's pleasure. A manuscript of 1349 described people picking their way down stinking lanes with their noses

The popular rose, beloved symbol of Love, Youth and Congratulations, emblem of England, was the favorite flower used to anchor the center of the tussie-mussie. The large, velvety petals were the perfect foil for smaller, frilly herbs and flowers placed around this important central flower. Roses were easy to come by, too, growing in every garden and readily available, now as then, from the florist.

buried in delicious nosegays. When they visited the sick to bleed or dose them, apothecaries and barber-surgeons carried aromatic tussie-mussies to guard against not just bad smells but disease itself. In law courts, a writer noted in 1649, rosemary and rue were placed on the judge's bench and the prisoners' dock to ward off gaol fever.

According to medieval logic, it was easy to determine which plant would cure a given disease. The so-called "Doctrine of Signatures" held that a plant's physical characteristics resembled the bodily part or disease that it cured. So aspen leaves, which trembled, cured palsy. Dandelion, with its milky sap, was good for nursing mothers; walnuts, with their convoluted meats, a cure for brain fever; the spotted lungwort, a prophylactic against tuberculosis. A related notion was that of "simples," which held that every plant could cure a specific ill. Thus thyme banished fatigue, lemon balm sharpened the wit, and sweetbriar made one cheerful. In time the herb became a symbol of the mental state to which it catered.

In the sixteenth century, medicinal nosegays began to give way to ornamental ones. Tussie-mussies sweetened the air, to be sure, and

In medieval paintings each flower represented had a special meaning. A lily, which symbolized the Virgin Birth, is found in almost every painting of the Annunciation, as we see in this 1425 Flemish altarpiece, below. Paintings of sacred events incorporated flowers to symbolize the moral content of the story—the violet meant Humility, the lily-of-the-valley, Purity, while the strawberry stood for Fruits of the Spirit or Rewards for Good Deeds.

perhaps even held contagion at bay, but they also served the same decorative purpose as jewels, fans and gloves. Just as Elizabethan necks were surrounded by great ruffs or standing lace-edged collars, so tussie-mussies were encircled by stiff lace collars of their own and carried in gloved hands, worn pinned to the chest or suspended on rich chains.

Herbals of the sixteenth and seventeenth centuries make frequent references to tussie-mussies with decorative or ornamental functions. In 1597, John Gerard wrote in his herbal about sweet William: "The floures are kept and sustained in gardens . . . to please the eye. They are . . . esteemed for their beauty, to deck up gardens and the bosoms of the beautiful, and garlands and crowns for pleasure." Cat's feet (pussy-toes), an easily dried everlasting, he wrote, was "a principal ornament for our belles."

John Parkinson, a gardener as well as a physician to King Charles I, wrote a book suggesting the symbolic use of herbs for "word posies" or "nosegayes with a message"— one of the earliest allusions to what would become a craze in the nineteenth century. "To make a delicate tussie-mussie, both for sight and scent," he recommended "yellow larkes spurs" (nasturtiums) and "gilliflowers" (carnations). In *Paradisi En Sole* he described the various flowers in his Garden of Pleasure and

Caged in her farthingale and stiff silks, the little Infanta Maria Theresa, whom Velázquez painted around 1660, clutches in one hand a tussie-mussie as stiffly ordered as her costume. Only the lavish handkerchief streaming from her other hand defies the rigor of Spanish court fashion.

advises the reader to "adde a few sweete herbes, both to accomplish the Garden, and to please your senses, by placing them in your Nosegayes, or elsewhere as you list." He particularly commends wallflowers: "The sweetness of the flowers causeth them to be generally used in Nosegayes."

As the Elizabethan Age drew to a close, flowers remained essential to a fashionable appearance. As the ruff was replaced by the soft lacy collar, tussie-mussies wore softer collars, too. In the court of Louis XIII, bouquets were pinned to the manliest chests. When low-cut necklines came into style, and stiff brocades were replaced by airy silks, fashion for a cultivated déshabille called for bosom flowers, with their sensual connotations.

By the mid-seventeenth century, the trend for flowers as costume accessories had increased dramatically. During the reign of Louis XIV highly stylized, oval boutonnieres were worn by men on their gorgeous pastel coats, and tussie-mussies were carried by both sexes. Tussies composed of herbs and flowers were tucked into fitted bodices. The flowers at Louis XIV's marriage to Maria Theresa of Austria in 1660 were tied with lavish ribbons, gold lace, bows and

The belief that a certain plant cured a specific emotional ill led to the development of the medieval language of herbs.

HERB	EMOTION
lemon balm	sharpen wit
catnip	relieve stress
pinks	relieve melancholy
borage	give courage
sage	bring wisdom
mint	provide refreshment
sweetbriar	bring cheer

❧ *Lemon balm*

rosettes. In England, after the Restoration of Charles II, the courtiers, who had spent weary years of exile in France, expressed an unbridled passion for scented lace handkerchiefs, perfumed gloves with embroidered gauntlets, long, curled wigs, floppy hats and, most importantly, enormous buttonhole bouquets "approaching the size of a cabbage."

Women, in their sweetheart necklines, silk skirts held out by farthingales, carried tussie-mussies wrapped in handkerchiefs or paper foil to keep their gloves clean. Since everyone could afford flowers, the style was enjoyed by all classes. Provincials and colonials carried tussie-mussies in their hands when they went visiting. Country folk wore them for weddings, fairs and church, just like the figures at court.

With the advent of the eighteenth century, flowers remained infinitely desirable, and artificial as well as fresh ones played a part. Fashionable women wore clusters of flowers on the left shoulder, on the sleeve, or pinned to one side of their low, square necklines. Garlands crossed the breast from shoulder to waist, trailed over the skirt or encircled the arm. Posies were fixed to fans and muffs. Little chaplets sat on the coiffure, with a central posy dipping over the forehead. The massive powdered

Flowers galore: The fragrant little tussie-mussie this swain offers his lady friend is all but eclipsed by the splendor of the embroidered bouquets flowing over the gorgeous gowns of the period.

In the eighteenth century, embroidery and needlepoint flowers, mixed with scrolls and fronds, embellished brocades and richly patterned silks. Painted silks from China, with beautifully detailed naturalistic flowers, came to Europe via India and became the vogue in France and England.

headdresses of the late century were decorated with feathers, ribbons, jewels and, of course, flowers. Later, as elegance gave way to a vogue for the simple and pastoral, women carried baskets of flowers over their arms, as if they had just returned from the garden.

In addition to playing leading roles in fashion and literature, flowers also played an important part in the scientific advances of the era. Hundreds of new plants were introduced to Europe from the New World and from Asia by plant hunters and explorers. Carl von Linnaeus, scholarly hero in Europe, was the celebrated author of a systematic method of plant classification based on the reproductive organs of flowers. His easy-to-understand system, "requiring no more than the ability to count to twelve," was largely responsible for the rage of amateur botanizing in the last half of the eighteenth century and the whole of the nineteenth. Linnaeus' focus on sexual flower parts caused a sensation; his metaphorical "loves of plants" was readily accepted into the robust culture of the 1700s, and people began to regard flowers from a sexual or romantic perspective. Science and romance intermingled. This frame of reference certainly contributed to the development of the Language of Flowers in the following century.

Godey's Lady's Book for February 1875 commends to its readers a plethora of flounces, bows, pleats, and in the case of this figure in pink evening dress, a veritable harness of rosy garlands and tussie-mussies.

VICTORIAN FLORAMANIA

The Golden
Age of the
Tussie-Mussie

THE HONEYSUCKLE *Periclymenum)*—

BONDS C

RECOLLECTIONS of childhood are chiefly associated wit
pleasurable incidents; hence the scenes mid which our golde
age was passed are ever bound round our heart by the fon
regard. Wander where we will over the wide world, for
many new ties as we may, ties the nearest and deares
the human heart can conceive of, pass through period
richest enjoyment that our being is capable of feel
is still—latent it may be in general—but there is st
strong, and abiding affection for that particular
native land where our early years were spent,
have expressed this, some poets in language
pressive, as, for instance, Scott:—

"Breathes there the man, with soul so de
Who never to himself hath said,
This is my own, my native land,"

and here we have the same feeling sho
lines with which our flower is woven;

"There the wild Honeysuckle, gat
In blending hues of yellow and
With rich abundance, thro
Their fragrant sweets upon
No blooming shrub's mor
Than Woodbine wild

Those Bonds of Love are, perh
bind the child to the parent,

PINK ROSEBUD.

Therefore with thy soft breath
come floating by
A thousand images
of love and grief,
Dreams, filled with
tokens of...

THE

HAND-BOOK

OF THE

Language and Sentiment of Flowers;

CONTAINING

THE NAME OF EVERY FLOWER TO WHICH
A SENTIMENT HAS BEEN ASSIGNED.

WITH

INTRODUCTORY OBSE...

By the Author of "...

Down in a green and
a modes... grew;

APPLE BLOSSOM.

Fair pledges of a fruitful tree.
Why do ye fall so fast?
Your date is not so past.
But you may stay yet here awhile
To blush and gently smile,
And go at last.

THE ROSE.—Beauty.

Moore rapturously sings of the Rose.—
Rose! thou art the sweetest flower,
that ever drank the amber shower;
Rose! thou art the fondest child
of dimpled Spring,
the wood-nymph wild!

Scarlet Ipomœa.— Honeysuckle.

I t was an age of flowers. When the queen who gave it her name was married in 1840, her wedding dress was embroidered with the plants of her realm: the Tudor rose of England, the leek of Wales, the shamrock of Ireland, the thistle of Scotland. In middle-class homes everywhere, the carpets were thick with roses; the paper on the walls was garlanded with them and strewn with violets and pansies. On the drawing room table blazed a bouquet of flowers from the garden, on the mantel a dried arrangement was protected from the humidity by a glass bell. From brackets hung baskets of creeping Jennie, sedum, tradescantia and clematis. In a window an elaborate case sheltered ferns, begonias and variegated ivy. In the garden outside, formal parterres had been dug up and replaced by flower beds shaped like tadpoles or stars scattered over the lawn and planted with one or at most two sorts of brilliantly colored flowers—red geraniums and blue lobelia, yellow calceolarias and purple pansies.

But not only the house and garden burgeoned with flowers. Those who trod those floral carpets and breathed that scented air adorned themselves unabashedly with posies.

❦ A tussie which includes chamomile (Initiative), larkspur (Swiftness) and poppy (Enthusiasm) spells Seize the Day! in flower language.

In their buttonholes men tucked rosebuds, carnations and orchids (though perhaps few emulated Oscar Wilde's sunflower). Women wore tussie-mussies in their hair, on their hats and bonnets, at the collar or in the décolletage of their dresses. They tied them to their wrists, pinned them to their voluminous skirts, carried them neatly bunched and tied with ribbon or inserted in a posy holder.

Barred from serious dirt gardening by their presumed delicacy and unsuitable costume, women more than made up for it by taking up botanical drawing and painting. Many albums of plant portraits—some of them exquisite— painted by Victorian ladies have survived. The subject of botany, considered so appropriate for young women, produced a spate of books beginning in 1781 with Rousseau's *Lettres Elementaires sur la Botanique*. A half-century later they were still appearing. John Lindley's *Lady's Botany* (1834) and Jane Loudon's *Botany for Ladies* (1842) went through several editions. In 1826, it was reported, a young lady was asked by a suitor about her bouquet. She gave him so confident a report of the common and Latin names of each flower that he was shamed into studying botany himself in order to be worthy of her.

Never had flowers been more gracefully incorporated into the art of living than in the Victorian era. The walls of aristocratic houses were hung with flowered tapestries, beds and windows were festooned with flowered silks and linen, while outside formal gardens displayed their floral beauties.

❧ *Queen Victoria at the Opera in 1837 carrying a tussie-mussie.*

❧ *Star magnolia buds (Sweetness), pear blossoms (Comfort) and grape hyacinths (Usefulness) make up a perfect tussie to give a helpful friend.*

By the dawn of the nineteenth century, fresh tussie-mussies, ever more artfully composed, were an essential part of every woman's costume. When the young Victoria ascended the throne in 1837, tussie-mussies were established as the key accessory and continued in popularity until the close of the century. Tussie-mussies were carried everywhere—on morning walks and picnics, to afternoon teas, dinners and dances. Soon they were indispensable at weddings. In the evening, these neat little nosegays were worn at the breast with stems thrust into a water-filled "bosom bottle" or carried in a posy holder. Even men were known to carry bouquets, as did the young swain who married General Grant's daughter in 1874. His pink and white bouquet had a small silver banner inscribed with the word "Love."

With the increasing popularity of the tussie-mussie, proficiency in the floral arts became a vital part of every young lady's education. Throughout much of the nineteenth century, young ladies were taught how to tie splendid tussie-mussies at home, following the directive of 1836: "Mothers should teach their daughters religion and the art of making a well-made hand bouquet." A simple, delightful occupation deemed suitable for the fair sex, its makings could be found in most flower gardens, and the crafting and giving of tussie-mussies was an everyday part of Victorian childhood.

In the latter half of the century, finishing schools took over the instruction and offered courses in "Flower Appreciation," which included botany, flower painting and the tying of tussie-mussies. "Florigraphy," or "the Language of Flowers," was also a vital part of the curriculum, in which each flower, herb, tree and shrub was assigned a meaning that had been developing in France since the Revolution and by the 1830s and '40s had become very popular in England and America. "The Language of Flowers has recently attracted so much attention," wrote the American writer Catherine Waterman in 1839, "that an acquaintance with it seems to be deemed, if not an essential part of a polite education, at least a graceful and elegant accomplishment." Flower language dictionaries to aid in the translation of tussie-mussies flooded the market. The properly instructed young lady should be able to decipher whatever coded message might lurk in the bouquet sent by an admirer. One unusual mention of this practice is provided in a letter from Gustave Flaubert to his mistress, written in 1846: "It gave you pleasure, poor angel, the name-day bouquet I sent you! It

In the Victorian era, proficiency in the floral arts became a vital part of a young lady's education. Finishing schools offered instruction in botany and "Florigraphy," or the "Language of Flowers," in which each flower, herb, tree and shrub was assigned a meaning. The Language of Flowers was deemed, if not an essential part of a polite education, at least a graceful accomplishment.

"And so, your daughter is at the Academy? How does she get along?"

"Splendidly; she's studying all the higher branches."

"Is she studying languages?"

"Oh, yes, she has nearly completed the Language of Flowers and is now engaged in the Language of Perfumes. My! What an education that girl will have."

—*Ladies Floral Cabinet* (1884)

45

In the Language of Flowers, little-leaf basil means Love and Best Wishes and columbine, I Cannot Give Thee Up.

wasn't my idea to put those eloquent flowers in my letter: I was unaware of their symbolic meaning. It was DuCamp who taught it to me and advised me to make use of it. I thought that bit of childishness would amuse your heart. It greatly amused mine."

Generations of young women were conversant with the meanings implied by ivy (Marriage), almond blossoms (Indiscretion), anemones (Forsaken!) and iris (Passion or, if one consulted a different dictionary, Eloquence). One characteristic all messages had in common was vague generality. "Fly away with me," a tussie-mussie might suggest, but never "Meet me at the railway depot at six-thirty."

Though generally carried in the hand, tussie-mussies were also worn as accessories by nineteenth-century women. In their homes, women hung them on chandeliers, tied them to banisters, displayed them in their three-legged posy holders on the mantel or table, and when out driving stuck them in holders mounted in the carriage—an amenity that survived into the age of the automobile.

There seemed to be no limit to the number of bouquets a girl might sport at a dance if she was popular. An American florist described a young lady "carrying a bouquet in each hand, while three others were strung from each arm as trophies of her prowess among the simpler, if not the softer sex." In the 1860s, florists in New

York sold bouquets for about five dollars; "extra fine" cost ten or even twenty dollars—the equivalent in today's terms of a rather handsome bit of jewelry. These tributes were either handed over by the admirer himself or delivered by messenger in a basket or zinc box, lined with moist moss. Those who were loath to invest ten dollars could buy their bouquets from street sellers for a fraction of that sum.

The nosegays a girl received from a man were no doubt made up by the florist or flower girl, but every Victorian young lady had to know how to make them herself. "Nothing requires more taste or skill than a well-made bouquet," wrote Annie Hassard, a Victorian floral designer and writer. No longer acceptable was a little bundle of herbs and flowers haphazardly bunched together. Tussie-mussies were subjected to severe evaluation at social functions: a bouquet badly executed or mistranslated reflected on a lady's judgment. "To get a half dozen of mixed flowers bundled together anyhow, and go into good company with such a nosegay, is looked upon as certainly not a mark of high breeding," warned *Godey's* in 1855. Detailed directives were published in prominent fashion magazines to spur on the fumbling posy maker. Thus an English writer described the composition of a single nosegay as "white roses interspersed with a mass of scarlet geraniums and surrounded by

Godey's Lady's Book speaks with relish of the flower girls who sold tussie-mussies for a few sous: "In the city the neat bouquets upon the market stalls indicate a growing taste among all classes . . . . There is not a prettier sight in the world than these bright young creatures, with their tasteful bouquets arranged in a light basket. They have a glance and a smile for every passerby, and a rose will be added for a trifling consideration."

POSY HOLDERS:

A Popular Collectible

Posy holders did what you might suppose. A cone- or cornucopia-shaped tube, often of gold or silver, held the stems of posies or tussie-mussies. A chain attached to the holder had a ring at the other end that slipped over the finger for safety.

Inside the lip a stout pin kept the tussie-mussie securely in place. The ingenious device functioned as a highly decorative handle for the tussie-mussie.

The holders were invented in France during the eighteenth century, when no costume was complete without fresh flowers worn as bou-

⚘ Gilt openwork holder with brilliant cobalt enamelled handle, c.1880.

⚘ Vermeil bosom vase with leaf and swirl motif.

tonnieres, tucked into the décolletage or carried in a dainty basket or in the hand.

In the 1730s the trade cards of Paris jewelers and Birmingham "toy men" showed little gold and silver glass-lined tubes that held fresh tussie-mussies. In the 1740s a spring-clip was added to fasten the holder to the costume. Posy holders that survive from this period reveal great individuality, artistic excellence and technical expertise.

Most posy holders were about four inches in length, half of which was a slim vase into which the flower stems fit neatly. Jewelers and goldsmiths rivaled one another in creating designs. The most striking innovation was the tripod, designed to permit a lady to set her posy holder on the table during dinner. The handle's end was so split that when a spring was released or a knob turned, three legs would pop out. The most costly posy holders were set with pearls, diamonds and rubies in designs suggesting flowers or fruit: turquoise, for example, arranged like forget-me-nots, coral beads mimicking berries, or garnets set like a bunch of grapes. Bezel settings were used for cabochon stones, Scotch pebbles, cameos and silhouettes. Tiny colored stones were inlaid in Florentine mosaics. Mirrors, medallions and lockets were sometimes added and there might even be a space for a portrait of the owner's fiancé, once he was won. Some were engraved with names, monograms or "word poesies" (rhyming couplets). Casting, embossing and repoussé achieved bas-relief effects—rich cabbage roses, pansies, grapes and oak leaves with acorns, butterflies and birds. Delicate holders were made of filigree and spun silver.

Today, posy holders are collected avidly. Fine specimens with handles of bone, coral or ivory are much sought after, as are mother-of-pearl handles

An especially fine specimen with carved ivory handle and inset turquoise stones.

(cool to the touch), amber ones (warm) and tortoiseshell. So are the fragile, charmingly painted porcelain holders, often from Dresden. The most costly holders were of gold. Because many were melted

An ingenious holder whose expandable legs make a tripod in which the bouquet can be displayed after the ball.

down after fashion abandoned them, they are now rare, but one may find sterling, vermeil (gold plate over sterling) and silver gilt (silver with a thin wash of gold). Pinchbeck or ormolu passed for gold if one didn't look too closely. Even Celluloid, invented in 1850, was made into modish posy holders. At the other end of the scale, Fabergé made posy holders of gold and enamel for the Russian imperial family—precious collectors' items indeed, yet perhaps not so charming as one of those ephemeral plaited- or woven-straw holders—just the thing for picnics.

High Fashion? This lady has a tussie-mussie fastened to the huge structure of false hair, ribbons and muslin balanced on her head, and another sprouting boldly from her bosom. The bristling tussie-mussie in her cleavage must have tickled.

half blown double white camellias. A very pretty bouquet for morning may be formed of white flowers surrounded by double violets. No bouquet is good without a rich green and a dead white."

By the 1860s, designers were advocating a regrouping of flowers, and concentric circles of flowers began to lose their charm. "The arrangement of colors in simple geometrical forms is preferable to a succession of distinct rings in a bouquet," counseled the well-known Brooklyn florist James Park.

Strong color contrasts were admired—orange next to blue, purple to yellow, green to red. "There is no doubt," *Godey's* pronounced with its customary conviction, "that arranging flowers according to their contrast or complementary colors is more pleasing to the eye than placing them according to their harmonies." The harmonies against which *Godey's* inveighed in the 1850s, however, became popular by the 1870s, in bouquets just as in flower beds. "As a practical rule in planting parterres," wrote an authority who might as well have been discussing posies, "the most intense colors should be placed in the center, gradually softening down towards the margin of the bed or the sides of the garden."

The bouquet, which depended for its success on the colors and the precision of the arrangement, often consisted of a large flower in the center (a rose or possibly a white Amazon lily) surrounded by rings of color (violets and geraniums, perhaps) and fringed with greenery (rose geranium) and "vandycked bouquet paper" or real lace. A good Victorian bouquet, like a good drawing room, must be crowded, and there was little effort to make a naturalistic arrangement or to give value to individual blossoms. The tightly packed heads were wired to slender twigs (their own stems being too frail to hold up to use) and wrapped in damp moss. The handle thus provided could be finished off with ribbon or put into a posy holder.

The bouquet's size varied from a small breast posy to "cartwheels" sixteen inches across—the larger, the more fashionable—and the time of day counted as well. Red carnations were for day wear, white for evening. In the morning a nosegay of sweet herbs might suffice; for excursions to the country, bunches of violets, daisies, forget-me-nots, wildflowers, berries and grasses were suitable. Afternoon tea called for a bouquet of garden flowers, and gala evenings for such arrangements as moss rosebuds surrounded by clove pinks, heliotropes, lemon verbena, mignonette and rose geranium.

Absolute rules, however, could

The female silhouette is almost like a large, inverted tussie-mussie. *Godey's Lady's Book* shows the fashions for January 1875. The belle in pink sports a tussie-mussie made up of tight concentric rings of flowers surrounding a central rose.

Toward the end of the nineteenth century, simplicity of design became associated with good taste and the formal tussie-mussie was largely supplanted by loose bunches of flowers with long, beautiful stems. These graceful "corsage bouquets" were composed of seasonal flowers chosen to duplicate the color of the lady's ensemble.

not last. Just as the practice of bedding plants in the garden gave way to looser, more informal herbaceous borders, bouquets made up of concentric rings of flowers, whether contrasting or harmonizing, began to lose their charm. Some people of taste, a writer observed, preferred to use their garden flowers to form what they called "old-fashioned English nosegays. Only sweet-scented blossoms were selected for such groupings: clove pinks and spicy carnations, fragrant white lilies and honeysuckle, reseda or mignonette, the flaunting cabbage rose, and the shy but beloved moss rose. The whole odorous collection was edged—not with . . . florist's lace paper—but with the airy spray of artemisia, a perfumed green lace of nature's own making."

Fashions changed as the century drew to a close. As early as 1866, a newspaper reported that "flowers for hair and dress are now very rarely mixed. As a general thing one flower with its own leaves is enough for one person's ambition." When the future Queen Mary was a bride in 1873, she carried a "shower bouquet" indicating the shape of things to come: an asymmetrical cascade of flowers trailing down to end in a single blossom. By the late 1880s, loose bunches of one or two kinds of long-stemmed flowers had supplanted the round tussie-mussie. Called "corsage bouquets," they were usually monochromatic, matching the wearer's dress.

Except at weddings, the twentieth century has seen precious little of posies, nosegays and bouquets, but now, after a century, the wheel has come full circle. The tussie-mussie of long ago is reappearing, a neat little nosegay of fragrant herbs and flowers, four or five inches across at most, which carries from maker to recipient a message of affection—sometimes quite specific, as we shall see.

❧ The late Victorian wedding bouquet of a few kinds of flowers indicated the shape of things to come.

Making a Tussie-Mussie

A Step-by-Step Guide

Who, having read this far, can resist trying her (or his) own hand at making a tussie-mussie? The possibilities are as limitless as your imagination, but here are a few pointers to help in your arrangement. If you intend to send a posy with a message, you can approach your composition by one of two avenues. Either you determine what plant materials are available—in the garden or on a country road, at the florist, or even the grocery store—and using the Glossary on page 133, decide how to arrange it in the most suitable manner. Or, on the other hand, you can figure out what you want to say and, with the assistance of the "Index of Sentiments" on page 145, determine which flowers will carry your message. All that remains is to find the needed flowers, compose your tussie-mussie and attach a card identifying the meanings of the flowers.

At the same time, it is important to think about the appearance and color of the flowers, choosing those that go well together. Since the most popular sentiments are generally expressed by a fairly wide choice of flowers, it shouldn't be hard to make substitutions when you can't find your first choice.

EQUIPMENT

Cutting the stems
scissors—to cut soft stems
garden clippers—to cut woody stems
utility shears—to cut wire and stems
long tweezers

Tying the bundle
four-ply woolen yarn—to bind stems together
florist's wire, fine
pipe cleaners

Finishing the handle
spaghnum moss, wrapped in plastic
florist's tape, waxed

Creating the holder
paper lace doilies—4, 5, or 6 inches across
short straight pins
florist's tape
real lace doilies (optional)
junior bouquet holders—if you're all thumbs

Trimming the tussie-mussie
ribbons, narrow—satin, moiré, taffeta, or grosgrain
embroidery scissors—to cut doilies, ribbons, thread and tiny sprigs of herbs

57

Almost anything can be used in making a tussie-mussie, but here is a list of flowers and herbs easy to handle and readily available.
Central flower: rosebud.
Small leaves and flowers for the concentric rings: baby's breath, tiny carnations, button mums, small asters, African violets, parsley, yarrow, rosemary, marjoram, lavender, feverfew, dried everlastings.
Leaves for the frame: fern ivy, galax, dustymiller, leaf lettuce, savoy cabbage, leaves of trees such as linden, oak and maple.
For a traditional tussiemussie: A central rose encircled by alyssum, forget-me-nots, marjoram, rosemary, clove pinks, Johnny-jump-ups, the whole framed with violet leaves.

To prepare the flowers and plants for your posy, strip off the lower leaves or branches. Then, with a clean, sharp knife or scissors, cut the stems on the diagonal and plunge them into tepid water to which you've added floral preservative. If the flowers are slightly overblown, put them in cold rather than tepid water. Leave them overnight in a cool, dark place (but not the refrigerator). Sometimes rosebuds with drooping necks, wilted heather or tired violets can be revived by submerging them overnight in tepid water. The stems of plants that ooze milky sap, such as milkweed, poppy, fern and euphorbia, should be singed in a flame or dipped in boiling water for a moment to make the sap coagulate. Some flowers, among them allium, delphinium and lupine, last longer if you turn them upside down and pour water into the hollow stems, plug them with a bit of cotton and put them in water.

Flower trusses with many blossoms, like tuberoses and miniature gladioli, may have unopened buds that you can remove with tweezers or embroidery scissors. If the florets are large, pull them apart and use them individually. This works especially well for lilies and gladioli.

1 With your fingers, strip any remaining leaves from the stems of the flowers and herbs. Using sharp clippers, shorten the stems to 4 or 5 inches, cutting on the diagonal.

2 Select a single important blossom for the center. A rosebud is traditional, but a tight bunch of lavender or any circular flower, like a daisy or calendula, will work nicely. Holding this flower in your left hand, surround it with 5 or 6 sprigs of a small, contrasting flower or herb, like blue cornflowers or thyme, adjusting the spacing as you go.

3 Add 2 or 3 more concentric rings of herbs and small flowers, shifting and adjusting so they are evenly spaced. With each successive ring, add 3 or 4 more flowers. To have good control of the tussie-mussie, bind the stems as you go. Using yarn, wire, pipe cleaners or florist's tape, bind the first ring of flowers in place around the center flower, making sure the flower tops are even. Wind the binding tightly down the stems.

4 Spiky flowers like lavender or veronica, or sprigs of the leaves of rosemary or marjoram contrast nicely with the smaller, rounder flowers. (Remember that a tussie-mussie differs from the standard bouquet in its generous use of greenery and fragrant herbs.) Five to 7 such sprigs will be about right for a 5-inch tussie-mussie. Bind them in place, a few at a time, spacing them evenly around the circle.

5 When the posy is 3 or 4 inches across, frame it with a circle of scented foliage, such as rose geranium, sage, artemisia, lamb's-ears or ivy. Finish binding the stems with pipe cleaners, yarn or tape, starting under the leaves and spiraling down the length of stems. Tie in the ends of yarn or string. If you used pipe cleaners or wire, push the ends into the stems; if florist's tape, stretch and blend the end into the finished handle. With clippers or utility shears, trim the stems to 3 or 4 inches.

6 If it is to be carried for quite a while, make a reservoir to keep the tussie-mussie fresh by pressing spaghnum moss soaked in water around the gathered stems or use a few layers of facial tissue cut to fit. When the moss or tissue is wet, cover it with plastic wrap or aluminum foil.

7 Finally, add a paper (or real) lace doily. Clip an X in the center by folding the doily in half for the first cut of 1 to 1½ inches, then refold it the other way for the second cut. Two doilies, one smaller than the other, add a nice touch. Be sure they stay dry, or they may tear when you put them in place.

8 Insert the bound stems into the opening in the doily, then slip the doily up so it rests against the underside of the foliage. Anchor it in place with small florist's pins before the next step.

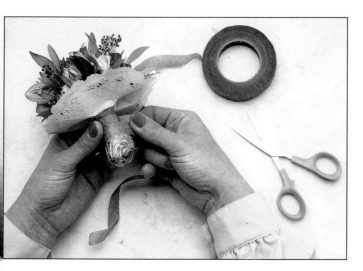

9 Wrap the stems with green or white florist's tape, stretching and overlapping it as you wind it diagonally down the stems. Catch the paper doily in the first loop or two and be sure to cover the moss, tissue, or plastic wrap completely, making a smooth, neat handle. Tie a bow on the handle, using 2 or 3 narrow ribbons that either match or contrast, and leave long streamers. Or, for a different message, make lover's knots at the ends.

HOLIDAYS
& FESTIVE
OCCASIONS

Happy Birthday to My Beloved

1 BASIL *Best Wishes*

2 PEACH *Longevity*

3 CHRYSANTHEMUM LEAF *Long Life, Joy, Optimism*

4 ROSE *Congratulations, Love*

5 LAVENDER *Success, Luck, Happiness*

6 IVY *Friendship*

7 PUSSY-TOES *Never-Ceasing Remembrance*

8 PLUM *Longevity*

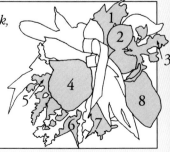

Baptism or Confirmation

1 COLUMBINE *Gifts of the Holy Spirit*

2 GARDEN ANEMONE LEAF *Faith, Belief*

3 THREE-LEAF CLOVER *The Trinity*

4 BLUEBERRY *Prayer*

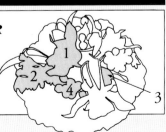

Happy Birthday to a Close Friend

1 PEACH *Longevity*

2 ROSE *Congratulations, Friendship*

3 LAVENDER *Luck, Success, Happiness*

4 BASIL *Best Wishes*

5 CHRYSANTHEMUM *Optimism, Joy, Long Life*

6 STATICE *Never-Ceasing Remembrance*

7 PLUM *Longevity*

Thank You!

1 BELLFLOWER *Gratitude*

2 LAVENDER *Acknowledgment*

3 PINK HYDRANGEA
Remembrance

4 DAISY FLEABANE *Thank You*

5 PARSLEY *Thanks, Gratitude*

6 PURPLE-LEAF SAGE
Gratitude

7 ROSEMARY
Remembrance

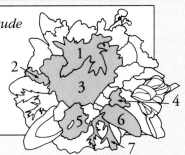

Belated Birthday or Anniversary

1 FORGET-ME-NOT
Do Not Forget Me!

2 SWEET MARJORAM *Blushes*

3 RED POPPY *Forgetfulness*

4 SWEET WILLIAM *Memory*

5 MINT *Warmth of Feeling*

6 BRAMBLE LEAF *Remorse*

7 JAPANESE ROSE *Never Too Late to Amend*

8 WOOD SORREL *Ill-Timed Wit*

9 SILVER-LEAF GERANIUM *Recall*

10 ASTER *Afterthought*

11 ROSEMARY *Remembrance*

12 COLTSFOOT *Justice Shall Be Done You*

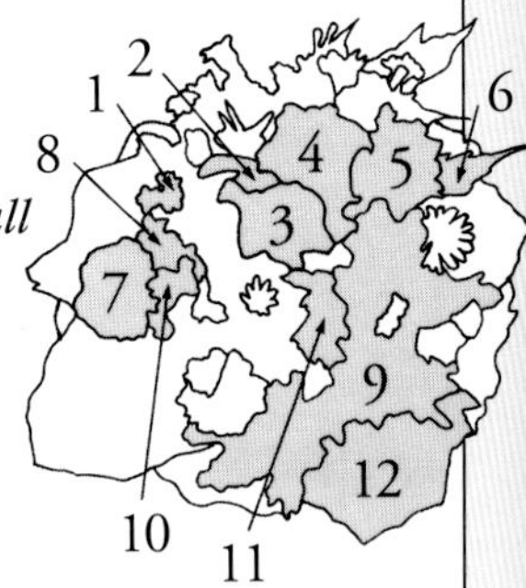

Sweet Sixteen

1 VARIEGATED TULIP *Beautiful Eyes*

2 FORGET-ME-NOT *Love*

3 BUGLE *Most Lovable, Cheers the Heart*

4 FOAMFLOWER *Attractive*

5 PANSY *Loving Thoughts*

6 DOGWOOD *Faithfulness*

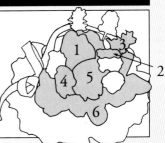

Bar/Bat Mitzvah

1 GOOSENECK LOOSESTRIFE
Wishes Granted

2 WHITE CLOVER *Luck*

3 RED ROSE *Victory, Joy, Love,*
Charm, Pride

4 MAGNOLIA *Perseverance*

5 VERVAIN *Good Fortune*

6 NUTMEG GERANIUM
An Expected Meeting

Mother's Day

1 FENNEL *Worthy of All Praise*

2 LEMON MINT *Virtue, Homeyness, Cheerfulness*

3 PURPLE CONEFLOWER *Skill, Capability*

4 GERANIUM *Comfort*

5 BEE BALM LEAF *Compassion, Sweet Virtues*

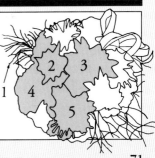

Father's Day

1 OAK *Steadfastness, Strength, Virtue*

2 PINEAPPLE MINT *Hospitality*

3 EAU DE COLOGNE MINT *Warmth of Feeling*

4 THYME FLOWER *Courage, Strength*

5 RED ROSE *Love*

6 LAVENDER *Devotion*

7 LAMB'S-EARS FLOWER *Gentleness, Support*

8 DOCK *Patience*

9 OXEYE DAISY *Patience*

10 SAGE *Wisdom*

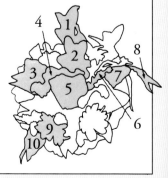

Christmas Joy

1 PINE *Warm Friendship, Vigorous Life, Spiritual Energy*

2 CINNAMON *Love, Beauty, My Fortune Is Yours!*

3 BURNET *A Merry Heart*

4 ROSEMARY *Remembrance*

5 BEDSTRAW *The Manger*

6 HOLLY BERRIES *Christmas Joy*

7 ROSE *Love*

8 CONE *Conviviality, Life*

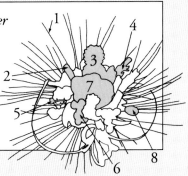

Valentine's Day

1 RED TULIP *Declaration of Love*

2 HONEYSUCKLE *Bonds of Love*

3 RED CARNATION *Passion, Fascination, Pure Love*

4 LARKSPUR *Ardent Attachment*

5 SILVER KING ARTEMISIA *Silver Moonlight, Unceasing Remembrance*

Sweetest Day

1 RUE *Grace*

2 COLUMBINE *I Cannot Give Thee Up!*

3 WEIGELA *Accept a Faithful Heart*

4 ROSEBUD *Confession of Love*

5 HEATHER *Admiration*

6 CARNATION *Admiration, You Are My Life!*

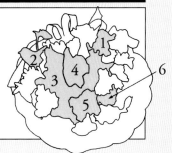

Sadie Hawkins Day

1 BORAGE *Bluntness, Directness, Speak Your Mind*

2 COCKSCOMB *Humor*

3 SNAPDRAGON *Dazzling But Dangerous*

4 PINKS *Boldness*

5 LAVENDER COTTON *Pursuit*

6 PERILLA *Role Reversal*

7 CHRYSANTHEMUM LEAF *Joviality, Mirth*

New Year's Resolutions

1 VERVAIN *Good Fortune, Wishes Granted*

2 SUMAC *Resoluteness*

3 RUE *Beginning Anew*

4 PARSLEY FLOWER *At the Very Beginning*

5 HYSSOP *Cleansing*

6 ELDERBERRY *Zeal*

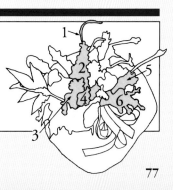

GOOD
HEALTH
&
RECOVERY

THOUGHTS OF YOU

To Your Health!

1 CALENDULA *Health, Constancy, The Sun*

2 BURNET *A Merry Heart*

3 FORGET-ME-NOT *Hope, Remembrance*

4 WALLFLOWER *Fidelity in Adversity*

5 FEVERFEW LEAF *Warmth, Good Health, You Light Up My Life!*

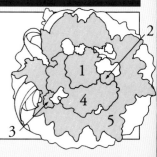

Congratulations on a Successful Diet

1 SWEET CICELY Gladness, Sincerity

2 ROSE Congratulations

3 FENNEL Thinness, To Grow Thin, Worthy of All Praise!

4 IVY Friendship

5 CHRYSANTHEMUM LEAF Optimism, Joy, Cheerfulness, Long Life

Get Well

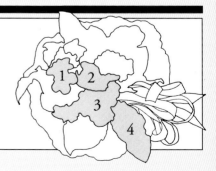

1 PLUMBAGO *Antidote*

2 ROSE *Love*

3 FEVERFEW *Good Health*

4 PUSSY WILLOW *Recovery from Illness*

Consolation for a Hangover

1 GILDED ROSE *Excess*

2 HEN-AND-CHICKENS *Welcome-Home-Husband-However-Drunk-Ye-Be*

3 POPPY MALLOW *Wine Cups*

4 HOPS *Beer, Mirth*

5 GRAPE *Carousing, Abandon*

6 BUTTERFLY BUSH *Rashness, Wantonness*

7 POKEWEED *A Jibe, Poking Fun*

8 MARIGOLD *Misery*

9 RED VALERIAN *Drunk and Blowsy*

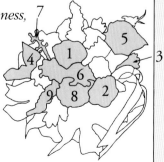

Convalescence after Surgery

1 CHAMOMILE *The Plant Physician*

2 ROSE *Love*

3 FORGET-ME-NOT *Hope*

4 YARROW *Heals Wounds, Health, Cure*

5 BACHELOR'S-BUTTON *Felicity, Healing Properties*

6 LAUREL *Success*

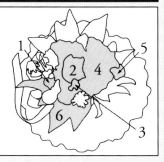

Recovery from Addiction

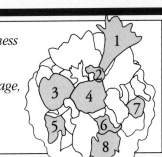

1 HOSTA *Devotion*

2 YARROW *Health*

3 GINGER *Safe, Pleasant, Comforting, Warming*

4 ROSE *Love*

5 BLUE SPIREA *Helpfulness*

6 SEDUM *Tranquility*

7 GARLIC CHIVES *Courage, Strength, Protection*

8 IMPATIENS *Felicity*

Consolation

1 GRASS *The Fleeting Quality of Life*

2 ROSEMARY *Remembrance*

3 WHITE ROSEBUD *A Heart Untouched by Love*

4 MARIGOLD *Grief*

5 STONECROP *Tranquility*

6 FLOWERING REED *Confidence in Heaven*

7 WOOD SORREL *Maternal Love*

8 ELDERBERRY *Sympathy, Kindness*

Sympathy during a Time of Grief

1 LEMON BALM *Sympathy*

2 THISTLE *Grief*

3 ROSEMARY *Remembrance*

4 ROSE *Love, Silence*

5 SWEET MARJORAM *Comfort, Consolation*

6 YEW *Sorrow*

7 RUE *Repentance and Grace*

8 SWEET WOODRUFF *Eternal Life*

9 MARIGOLD *Grief*

10 PRIMROSE LEAF *Sorrow*

11 SAGE *Mitigates Grief*

12 DEAD LEAVES *Sadness*

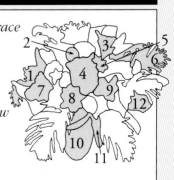

Comfort for Terminal Illness

1 TULIP *Happy Years, Memory*

2 STATICE *Sympathy*

3 LEMON BALM *Sympathy, Love,*
Relief

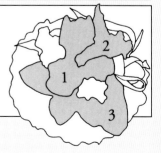

Recovering from Depression

1 WILLOW *Calmness, Serenity*

2 ARBORVITAE *Unchanging Friendship*

3 ELDERBERRY *Kindness*

4 LENTEN ROSE LEAF *Remedy for Madness*

5 PANSY *Loving Thoughts*

6 ROSE *Love, Friendship, You Are Gentle*

7 DELPHINIUM SEED PAD *Well-Being*

8 FEVERFEW *Health*

9 LEMON BALM *Drives Away Heaviness of Mind, Sharpens Wit*

10 GOLDENROD LEAF *Encouragement*

11 LAMB'S-EARS *Support*

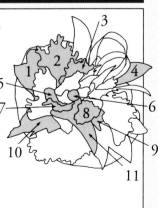

FRIENDSHIP

&

ROMANCE

Puppy Love

1 WHITE AZALEA *First Love*

2 FORGET-ME-NOT *True Love*

3 ENGLISH DAISY *Innocence, Simplicity*

4 THORNLESS ROSE *Early Attachment*

5 BUGLE *Most Lovable*

6 HOSTA *Devotion*

7 LILAC *First Emotions of Love*

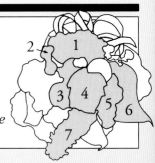

Infatuation

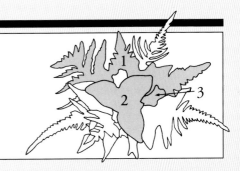

1 FERN *Fascination*

2 TIGER FLOWER *For Once May Pride Befriend Me!*

3 RAGWORT *I Am Humble But Proud!*

Secret Tryst

1 TUBEROSE *Dangerous Love, Voluptuousness*

2 RED ROSE *Passion, Love*

3 ROSEMARY *Remembrance*

4 ROSE GERANIUM *Preference*

5 NUTMEG GERANIUM *An Expected Meeting*

6 FORGET-ME-NOT *Do Not Forget Me!*

7 PENNYROYAL *Flee*

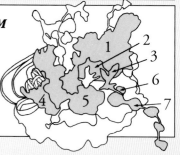

Engagement

1 BLEEDING HEART *Fidelity*

2 WHITE ROSE *Unity, Love, Beauty*

3 FORGET-ME-NOT *True Love*

4 WHITE AZALEA *Romance*

5 BRIDAL WREATH SPIREA
Victory

6 HOSTA *Devotion*

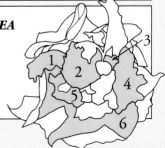

Flirtation

1 BUTTERCUP *Rich in Charms*

2 FEVERFEW *Flirt*

3 DAYLILY *Coquette*

4 BLACKBERRY *Dangerous Pride*

5 NIGELLA *Kiss Me Twice Before I Rise*

6 JERUSALEM SAGE *Earthly Delights*

7 BERGAMOT *Your Wiles Are Irresistible*

Wedding

1 LAVENDER *Devotion*

2 SWEET MARJORAM *Joy and Happiness*

3 LINDEN *Marital Virtues, Conjugal Love*

4 ORANGE BLOSSOMS *Bridal Festivities, Marriage, Fecundity*

5 ROSE *Unity, Love*

6 MYRTLE *Married Bliss, Fidelity, Love, Passion, Home*

7 HEARTSEASE *Happy Thoughts*

8 RUE *Vision, Virtue, Virginity*

9 HONEYSUCKLE *Bonds of Love, Generous and Devoted Affection, Devotion*

Anniversary Toast

1 CARAWAY *Love Charm to Prevent Infidelity*

2 DAFFODIL *Regard, Respect*

3 GOLDEN EUONYMUS *Long Life*

4 PLUM BLOSSOMS *Courage, Hardiness, Happiness, Marriage*

5 DOGWOOD *Love Unchanged by Adversity*

6 IVY *Wedded Love, Constancy*

Support during a Difficult Divorce

1 THISTLE *Defiance, Vengeance, Retaliation*

2 JAPANESE ANEMONE *Refusal, Abandonment*

3 MANDEVILLA *Reckless, Thoughtless*

4 CHASTE BUSH *Coldness, Indifference*

5 RAGWEED *Nuisance*

6 DAHLIA *Treachery, Instability, Misrepresentation*

Platonic Friendship/Camaraderie

1 FORSYTHIA *Good Nature*

2 PUSSY WILLOW *Friendship*

3 BLUE HYACINTH *Kindliness, Sport*

4 WORMWOOD *Affection*

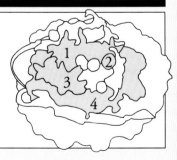

Consolation for a Broken Heart

1 LEMON BALM *Sympathy, Healing, Drives Away Heaviness of Mind*

2 LAVENDER *Soothes the Tremblings and Passions of the Heart*

3 ELDERBERRY *Kindness, Sympathy*

4 ROSE *Friendship, May You Be Pleased and Your Sorrows Mine!*

5 SENSITIVE PLANT *Sensibility, Be Careful, Do Not Hurt Me!*

6 PINK YARROW *Cure for Heartache, Dispels Melancholy, Health*

7 WILLOW *Serenity*

8 LENTEN ROSE *Cure for Melancholy*

Come Back Soon

1 SCENTED GERANIUM
Preference, Comfort

2 QUEEN ANNE'S LACE *I'll
Return, Haven, Home, Comfort*

3 BALLOON FLOWER *Return of a
Friend Is Desired*

4 ROSE *Love, Grace*

5 BELLFLOWER *Constancy,
Gratitude, Return of a
Friend Is Desired*

6 DELPHINIUM *Well-Being,
Sweetness, Beauty, Return of
a Friend Is Desired*

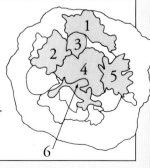

Conceiving a Child

1 TANSY *To Stay Miscarriages*

2 CREEPING JENNIE *Womb Plant*

3 PLUM *Fertility*

4 PINE CONE *Fertility, Life, The Testes*

5 VERBENA *Fertility*

6 MUGWORT *Helps Conception*

7 FIG *Fecundity, The Womb*

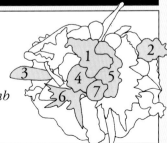

CELEBRATING

SPECIAL

PEOPLE

Honoring a Mentor

1 PERENNIAL BACHELOR'S-BUTTON *Felicity, Health*

2 SAGE FLOWER *Esteem, Wisdom*

3 STOCK *Lasting Beauty*

4 CLEMATIS *Mental Beauty, Unchanged for Eternity*

5 PRINCESS TREE *Benevolence*

6 LEMON BALM *Rejuvenation, Sharpens Wit*

Welcome to a Special Guest

1 PINEAPPLE MINT FLOWER
Welcome

2 SAGE Esteem

3 CARDINAL FLOWER Distinction,
Splendor

4 PEACOCK ORCHID
Distinction

5 CALADIUM Great Joy
and Delight

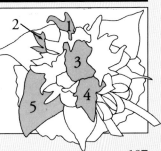

Rising Star/Prima Donna

1 CALLA LILY *Panache, Magnificent Beauty*

2 BLEEDING HEART *Elegance*

3 DAYLILY *Coquetry*

4 ROCKET *Fashionable, Vanity, Queen of Coquettes*

5 FUCHSIA *Taste*

6 HONEY LOCUST *Elegance*

Admiring a Creative Talent

1 MORNING GLORY *Evanescent*
   Loveliness of Life

2 CALLA LILY *Panache*

3 SAGE *Esteem*

4 PINKS *Talent*

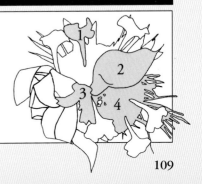

Welcome Back Soldier or Sailor

1 ZINNIA *Thoughts of Absent Friends*

2 STATICE *Dauntlessness*

3 STRAWFLOWER *Never-Ceasing Remembrance*

4 DOGWOOD FRUIT *Love in Adversity*

5 HARDY AGERATUM *Delay*

6 IVY *Friendship*

New Baby Girl

1 PEACH BLOSSOM *Feminine Softness*

2 PINK CARNATION *Maternal Love, Pride, Beauty*

3 CAMELLIA *Excellence, Beauty, Perfected Loveliness*

4 DANDELION SEED HEAD *Wishes Come True*

5 RUE *Grace*

6 SALAD BURNET *A Merry Heart*

7 LAVENDER *Luck!*

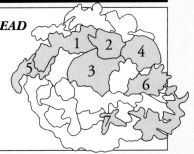

Newborn Boy

1 SALAD BURNET *Joy*

2 FEVERFEW *Health*

3 SORREL *Joy*

4 ROSE *Joy*

5 ENGLISH DAISY *Newborn Baby,*
Innocence

6 BABY'S BREATH *Pure Heart*

7 JAPANESE MAPLE *Baby's Hands*

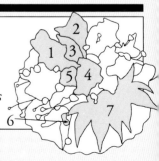

In Praise of Children

1 SWEET WILLIAM LEAF
Childhood

2 PINK ROSEBUD *A Young Girl,*
Beauty, Youth

3 ENGLISH DAISY *Simplicity,*
Innocence

4 YELLOW PRIMROSE *Early*
Youth, Innocence, Gaiety

5 GERANIUM LEAF *Childhood*

6 DAFFODIL *Gracefulness*

7 PINKS LEAF *Sweetness*

8 CLOVER *Good Education,*
Good Luck

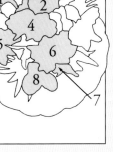

NEW
BEGINNINGS &
CONGRATULATIONS

Challenging a Rival

1 LAVENDER *Distrust*	**5 SINGLE PINKS** *Aversion*
2 ROCKET *Rivalry*	**6 SWEET WILLIAM** *Craftiness*
3 BASIL *Hatred*	**7 RUSSIAN OLIVE** *Bitterness*
4 MARIGOLD *Jealousy*	**8 RUE** *Disdain*

Embarking on a New Adventure

---

1 LAURUSTINUS *Thoughts of Heaven*

2 SWEET MARJORAM *Kindness, Courtesy*

3 PEAR *Hope, Benevolent Justice*

4 ENGLISH DAISY *Cheerfulness, Popular Oracle*

5 HEATHER *Wishes Come True, Protection From Danger*

6 IVY *Trustfulness*

Congratulations on Your Promotion

1 LAUREL *Personal Achievement*

2 BLUE SALVIA *I Think Of You!*

3 WHITE PINKS *Departure*

4 BASIL *Best Wishes*

5 DEAD NETTLE *Preferred*

6 ROSE *Congratulations*

7 ARBORVITAE *Friendship*

8 ROSEMARY *Remembrance*

9 PANSY *Thoughts*

10 SCENTED GERANIUM *Preference*

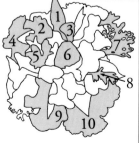

Welcome to Your New Home

1 OAK *Hospitality*

2 COMFREY *Home Sweet Home*

3 LAVENDER *Luck*

4 THYME *Activity*

5 TREFOIL *Providence*

6 SCARLET GERANIUM *Comfort*

7 ORANGE BLOSSOMS
Generosity, Happy Outcome

8 HORSE CHESTNUT *Luxury*

9 BROOM *Safety*

Invocation to the Muses/Creative Inspiration

1 LAUREL *Glory, Achievement in the Arts, Reward of Merit*

2 CAMELLIA *Excellence*

3 ACANTHUS *The Arts*

4 GLOBE AMARANTH *Immortality*

5 LUPINE *Imagination*

6 CORAL ROSE *Beauty, I Admire Your Accomplishments*

7 PLANE TREE *Genius*

8 WHITE PINKS *Talent, Ingeniousness*

9 TULIP POPLAR *Fame*

10 CREPE MYRTLE *Eloquence*

11 ANGELICA *Inspiration*

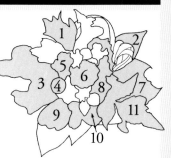

Congratulations on Your College Acceptance

1 CHERRY LEAF *Good Education*

2 ORCHID *Scholarship*

3 WALNUT *Intellect, Strength of Mind*

4 BORAGE *Courage*

5 ROSE *Congratulations*

6 CORAL BELLS *Hard Work, Industry, Challenge, Scholarship*

7 WOOD SORREL *Joys to Come*

8 BAYBERRY *Instruction*

9 LEMON BALM *Increases Memory, Sharpens Wit and Understanding*

Congratulations on Your College Graduation

1 CORAL BELLS *Hard Work, Industry*

2 SUMAC *Intellectual Excellence*

3 ROSE *Congratulations*

4 SAGE *Wisdom*

5 CHRYSANTHEMUM *Optimism*

6 WALNUT *Intellect, Strength of Mind*

7 LAUREL *Success, Reward of Merit*

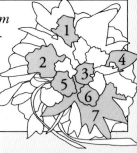

Good Luck on Your Job Application

1 VERVAIN *Good Fortune*

2 BUDS *Promise of Good Things to Come*

3 CREPE MYRTLE *Eloquence*

4 CLOVER *Luck*

5 PINK CONEFLOWER *Skill, Capability*

6 LAVENDER *Luck*

7 IVY *Ambition, Tenacity*

Great New Wheels!

1 ASTILBE *Worldly Pleasures*

2 AURICULA LEAF *Pride of Newly-Acquired Fortune*

3 SPIREA *Conceit, Self-Love*

4 JERUSALEM SAGE *Pride of Ownership, Earthly Delights*

5 RED GERANIUM *Comfort*

6 WILLOW FLOWER *Freedom*

7 WHITE PINKS *Mobility*

8 GLOSSY ABELIA *Sleekness*

Starting a New Garden

1 HOLLY *Foresight*

2 FORGET-ME-NOT *High Hopes*

3 JERUSALEM SAGE *Earthly Delights*

4 QUEEN OF THE PRAIRIE *Farsighted Outlook*

5 BUDS *Promise of Good Things to Come*

6 ANEMONE *Expectation*

7 CLOVER *Hard Work, Industry, Luck*

8 LAUREL *Personal Achievement*

9 PEONY *Beauty*

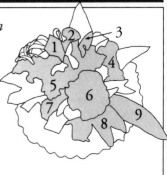

New Business Venture

1 LAUREL *Success*

2 PEONY *Hands Full of Cash*

3 SAGE FLOWERS *Wisdom*

4 HONESTY LEAF *Trustworthiness*

5 LOVAGE *Strength*

6 MOUNTAIN LAUREL *Ambition*

7 LAVENDER *Luck, Loyalty*

8 CLOVER *Luck*

9 THYME *Courage, Bravery*

10 WHITE PINKS *Ingenuity*

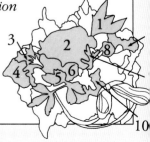

Go for the Gold!

1 HYACINTH *Games, Sports*

2 PINE *Endurance*

3 COLUMBINE *Resolved to Win*

4 ROCKET *Rivalry*

5 PINKS *Boldness*

6 MOUNTAIN LAUREL *Ambition*

7 CHAMOMILE *Energy in Adversity*

8 THYME *Activity*

9 CORAL BELLS
Challenge

10 BAMBOO *Strength,
Valor, Luck*

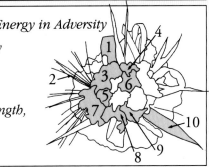

Your Efforts Will Pay Off

1 PURPLE-LEAF PLUM *Courage, Hardiness, Perseverance*

2 PERUVIAN LILY *Friendship, Pleasantries*

3 ROSE *Reward of Virtue*

4 GERANIUM *Health, Comfort*

5 MARIGOLD *Joy, Cares*

Eureka!

1 ROSE *Congratulations*

2 LAVENDER *Luck*

3 MAGNOLIA *Perseverance*

4 RUE *Vision*

5 CORAL BELLS LEAF *Hard Work*

6 SWEET AUTUMN CLEMATIS
Ingenuity, Mental Excellence

7 PEACOCK ORCHID
Distinction

8 STRAWBERRY BEGONIA
Cleverness

Bon Voyage

1 CAROLINA JASMINE LEAF
Separation

2 PENNYROYAL *Flee Away*

3 SPRUCE *Farewell*

4 LAVENDER COTTON *Wards Off Evil*

5 SWEET PEA *Departure*

6 PLANTAIN FLOWER *Well-Trodden Path, Pilgrimage*

7 CHAMOMILE *Help Against Wearisomeness, Patience, Comfort*

8 MUGWORT *Comfort, Prevents Tiredness, Be Not Weary!*

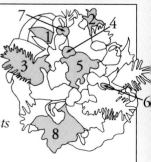

First Day in a New School/Job/City

1 SWEET MARJORAM *Mirth*

2 ROSE *Love*

3 CARNATION *Admiration, Fascination*

4 KALANCHOE *Popularity*

5 CLOVER *Good Luck*

6 CHRYSANTHEMUM *Cheerfulness*

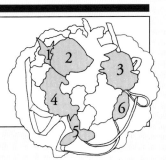

GLOSSARY

*Vocabulary of
Flowers*

A❀

+abelia, glossy .... *sleekness*
+acanthus.............................. *the Arts*
agapanthus/lily-of-the-Nile ... *love letters*
+ageratum, hardy.................. *delay*
allium/flowering onion .... *unity, humility, patience*
almond.................................. *hope, lover's charm, heedlessness*
alyssum, sweet...................... *worth beyond beauty*
+amaranth, globe.................. *immortality*
amaryllis............................... *splendid beauty, pride, haughtiness*
+anemone............................ *truth, sincerity, abandonment, expectation*
+anemone, garden................. *faith, belief*
+anemone, Japanese .... *refusal, abandonment*
+angelica.............................. *inspiration*
anthurium/flamingo flower ... *the heart, little boy flower*
apple .... *preference, fame speaks him great and good, perpetual concord, temptation*
+arborvitae............................ *unchanging friendship, tree of life*
+artemisia, Silver King .... *power, dignity, silver moonlight, sentimental recollections, unceasing remembrance*
+aster.................................... *variety, afterthought, beauty in retirement, sentimental recollections*
aster, double .... *I share your sentiments*
aster, Monte Cristo .... *enthusiasm*
aster, single .... *I will think of it*
+astilbe.................................. *I'll still be waiting, worldly pleasures*

+auricula/primula .... *pride of newly-acquired fortune*
+azalea .... *love, romance, first love, moderation*

B❀

+baby's breath .... *pure heart, festivity, gaiety*
+bachelor's-button/cornflower .... *felicity, healing properties, delicacy*
+balloon flower/platycodon............................ *return of a friend is desired*
+balm, lemon........................ *sharpens wit and understanding, healing, love, fun, relief, rejuvenation, social intercourse, sympathy*
+balsam/impatiens .... *ardent love, impatience, felicity*
+bamboo............................... *loyalty, steadfastness, uprightness, strength through pliancy*
+basil.................................... *best wishes, hatred*
+bayberry/wax myrtle .... *good luck, instruction*
bedstraw .... *Jesus' manger herb*
+bee balm/Monarda .... *compassion, sweet virtues, Your whims are quite unbearable!*
begonia .... *highly popular, long beautiful, unrequited love, Beware, I am fanciful!*
+begonia, strawberry/saxifrage .... *cleverness*
+bellflower/campanula .... *gratitude, constancy, aspiring, return of a friend is desired*
bells-of-Ireland .... *whimsy*

+means flower is pictured in one of the 60 tussie-mussies chosen for book

+bergamot............................ *Your wiles are irresistible!*

bittersweet .... *truth*

+blackberry........................... *dangerous pride*

black-eyed Susan.................. *justice*

+bleeding heart..................... *elegance, fidelity*

+blueberry .... *prayer, protection*

+borage................................. *courage, bluntness, directness, speak your mind*

bouvardia.............................. *enthusiasm*

box .... *stoicism*

+bramble............................... *remorse*

+broom/cystis, genista .... *humility, safety*

+buds .... *promise of good things to come*

+bugle/ajuga......................... *cheers the heart, most lovable*

+burnet, salad .... *a merry heart, joy*

+buttercup .... *rich in charms, cheerfulness, childishness, ingratitude*

+butterfly bush/buddlea........ *rashness, wantonness*

C

+caladium .... *great joy and delight*

+calendula/pot marigold....... *health, joy, remembrance, constancy, the sun, affection, disquietude, grief, jealousy, misery, cares*

+calla lily............................... *magnificent beauty, panache, feminine modesty*

+camellia............................... *excellence, beauty, perfected loveliness, contentment*

+candytuft............................. *indifference*

+caraway............................... *infidelity prevented*

+cardinal flower.................... *distinction and splendor*

+carnation............................. *admiration, fascination, ardent and pure love, bonds of love, unfading beauty, woman's love*

carnation, laced .... *passion*

+carnation, pink................... *maternal love, lively and pure affection, beauty, pride*

+carnation, red..................... *admiration, betrothal, deep pure love, passion, fascination*

carnation, striped................ *refusal*

carnation, white................... *democracy, living for love*

+carnation, yellow .... *admiration, fascination, disdain, I do not believe you, rejection*

+chamomile .... *energy in adversity, comfort, patience, the plant physician, help against wearisomeness*

+chaste bush/vitex............... *coldness, indifference*

+cherry................................. *sweetness of character derived from good works, good education, insincerity*

cherry, flowering .... *nobility, chivalry*

+chestnut, horse .... *luxury*

chickweed............................. *rendezvous*

+chives, garlic .... *courage, strength, protection*

+chrysanthemum................... *cheerfulness, optimism, long life, joy, joviality, mirth*

chrysanthemum, red............. *I love you*

chrysanthemum, white.......... *truth*

chrysanthemum, yellow .... *cheerfulness, slighted love*

+cicely, sweet .... *gladness, sincerity, rejoices and comforts the heart*

+cinnamon .... *love, beauty,*
My fortune is yours!

cinquefoil .... *maternal affection,*
beloved daughter

+clematis .... *mental beauty, inge-*
nuity, unchanged for
eternity, artifice

+clover .... *good luck, good edu-*
cation, hard work,
industry

+clover, three-leaf .... *the Trinity*

+clover, white .... *luck*

+cockscomb/celosia .... *silliness, humor*

+coltsfoot .... *Justice shall be done*
you

+columbine .... *I cannot give Thee*
up!, resolved to win,
gifts of the Holy Spirit,
folly, desertion

+comfrey .... *Home sweet home*

+cone .... *conviviality, life*

+coneflower .... *skill, capability*

+coral bells .... *challenge, scholar-*
ship, hard work,
dainty pleasures

coreopsis .... *always cheerful*

corn .... *riches,*
gift of Mother Earth

+cornflower/
bachelor's-button .... *delicacy, felicity,*
healing properties

cosmos .... *modesty, pure love of*
a virgin

+creeping Jennie/
lysimachia .... *forgiveness,*
womb plant

crocus .... *youthful gladness,*
pleasure of hope

crocus, saffron .... *Do not abuse, Beware*
of excess, mirth

cyclamen .... *diffidence, distrust,*
voluptuousness

cyclamen, light-colored .... *I understand you*

cyclamen, red .... *I will not economize*

cyclamen, white .... *warmhearted*

D

+daffodil .... *regard, respect,*
chivalry, gracefulness

+dahlia .... *gratitude, dignity,*
pomp, My gratitude
exceeds your care,
instability,
misrepresentation

dahlia, double .... *participation*

dahlia, single .... *good taste*

dahlia, variegated .... *I think of you*
constantly!

dahlia, white .... *gratitude to parents*

dahlia, yellow .... *I am happy that you*
love me!

daisy .... *innocence, simplicity*

+daisy, English .... *innocence, simplicity,*
newborn baby, cheer-
fulness, popular
oracle, I share your
sentiments

daisy, gerbera .... *sadness, needing pro-*
tection, friendship

+daisy, oxeye .... *a token of affection,*
patience

daisy, wreath of .... *I will think of it*

+daisy fleabane .... *thank you*

+dandelion .... *wishes come true,*
love's oracle

+daylily .... *coquette, flirt, beauty*

+dead leaves .... *sadness, melancholy*

+delphinium .... *well-being, sweetness,*
beauty, return of a
friend is desired

dill .... *irresistible, soothing*

dittany .... *birth*

+dock .... *patience*

+dogwood .... *love undiminished by*
adversity, faithfulness

dusty-miller .... *felicity, delicacy,*
venerable,
industriousness

135

E

+elderberry .... *kindness, compassion, zeal*

+euonymus/spindle tree .... *Your image is engraven on my heart, long life*

F

+fennel .... *worthy of all praise, force, strength, to grow thin, thinness*

+fern.................................... *fascination, sincerity*

fern, asparagus..................... *airy grace*

fern, maidenhair .... *discretion*

fern, walking .... *mobility*

+feverfew .... *good health, warmth, You light up my life!, flirt*

+fig .... *fecundity, the womb, longevity, peace and prosperity*

fleur-de-lis/iris .... *ardor, flame, message, eloquence, promise, My compliments*

+foamflower .... *attractive*

+forget-me-not...................... *true love, hope, remembrance, Do not forget me!*

+forsythia .... *good nature*

four o'clock/marvel of Peru... *timidity*

foxglove .... *insincerity, a wish, decision, I am not ambitious for myself but for you*

freesia.................................. *innocence*

+fuchsia............................... *taste*

G

galax.................................... *friendship, encouragement*

gardenia .... *transport of joy, ecstasy, I love you in secret, feminine charm, purity, peace*

garlic .... *protection, strength, courage, good luck*

gay-feather/liatris................. *gaiety*

gentian .... *loveliness, righteousness, You are unjust*

+geranium............................ *comfort, conjugal affection, You are childish!, melancholy, deceit, stupidity, childhood, health*

geranium, apple-scented .... *present preference*

geranium, ivy .... *bridal favor, I engage you for the next dance*

geranium, lemon-scented...... *unexpected meeting*

+geranium, nutmeg-scented .... *expected meeting*

geranium, penciled or skeleton .... *ingenuity*

geranium, pink .... *preference*

+geranium, red .... *comfort, health, protection*

+geranium, rose-scented .... *preference*

+geranium, scarlet .... *comfort, consolation, Your smile bewitches me!, folly, stupidity*

+geranium, scented .... *gentility, preference, comfort*

+geranium, silver-leaf........... *recall*

geranium, white.................... *gracefulness*

geranium, wild or hardy .... *constancy, availability, I desire to please, envy*

+ginger................................. *safe, pleasant, comforting, warming* gladiolus.............................. *generosity, strength of character, You pierce my heart!*

globeflower/trollius............... *solitude, generosity, gratitude*

+goldenrod .... *encouragement, precaution, good fortune*

+grape.................................. *carousing, abandon, intoxication, prosperity and plenty, domestic happiness*

+grass................................... *the fleeting quality of life, submission*

H

+heartsease/
Johnny-jump-up .... *happy thoughts*

+heather................................ *admiration, wishes come true, protection from danger*

heather, white....................... *good luck*

+hen-and-chickens/sedum.... *welcome-home-husband-however-drunk-ye-be*

+holly.................................... *foresight, good will, domestic happiness*

holly, sea/eryngium............... *graceful, attractive, traveler's luck*

+holly berries........................ *Christmas joy, protection*

hollyhock.............................. *fruitfulness*

hollyhock, white.................... *female ambition*

+honesty .... *trustworthiness, sincerity*

+honeysuckle .... *bonds of love, generous and devoted affection*

+hops.................................... *beer, mirth, rest, sleep*

+hosta .... *devotion*

+hyacinth .... *play, games, sport*

+hyacinth, blue...................... *kindliness, sport*

hyacinth, grape .... *usefulness*

+hydrangea .... *devotion, remembrance, boastfulness*

+hyssop................................. *cleansing*

I

ice plant .... *Your looks freeze me!, rejected suitor*

+impatiens/balsam .... *felicity, impatience*

iris/fleur-de-lis .... *message, eloquence, promise, My compliments, ardor, flame*

+ivy .... *wedded love, fidelity, constancy, friendship, trustfulness, ambition, tenacity*

J

jasmine .... *transport of joy, amiability*

+jasmine, Carolina .... *grace, elegance, separation*

+Johnny-jump-up/
heartsease .... *happy thoughts*

jonquil.................................. *I desire a return of affection, Have pity on my passion!*

juniper.................................. *welcome to new home, protection, asylum*

K

+kalanchoe .... *popularity*

L

lady's slipper......................... *capricious beauty, fickleness*

+lamb's-ears .... *softness, gentleness, surprise, support*

+larkspur .... *ardent attachment, levity, swiftness*

larkspur, double .... *haughtiness*

larkspur, pink .... *fickleness*

+laurel .... *success, personal achievement, glory, achievement in the Arts, reward of merit, accomplishment*

+laurustinus/viburnum .... *I die if neglected!, a token of affection, thoughts of heaven*

+lavender .... *devotion, luck, success, happiness, distrust, soothes the tremblings and passions of the heart, ardent attachment*

+lavender cotton .... *aggressiveness, pursuit, wards off evil*

lemon .... *fidelity in love, zeal, discretion*

+lilac .... *youth, acceptance, love, beauty, modesty*

lilac, purple .... *first emotions of love*

lilac, white .... *youthful innocence, purity, sweetness*

lily .... *purity, fruitfulness, majesty, resurrection*

lily, blackberry .... *thriving*

lily, foxtail .... *aspiration*

lily, Japanese .... *You cannot deceive me*

lily, Peruvian/alstromeria ...... *friendship, pleasantries*

lily, scarlet .... *high-souled*

lily, tiger .... *wealth, pride*

lily, Turk's-cap .... *splendor*

lily, yellow .... *gaiety, falsehood, coquetry*

lily-of-the-valley .... *return of happiness, purity, delicacy*

+linden/tillia .... *conjugal love, marital virtues*

lisianthus .... *showy*

locust .... *elegance*

+loosestrife, gooseneck .... *wishes granted, forgiveness*

+lovage .... *strength*

love-lies-bleeding/
amaranthus .... *hopeless, not heartless*

+lupine .... *imagination, voraciousness*

M

+magnolia .... *sweetness, beauty, perseverance*

+mandevilla .... *reckless, thoughtless*

+maple .... *reserve, elegance, keys, beauty*

+maple, Japanese .... *baby's hands*

+marigold, pot/calendula ...... *health, joy, remembrance, constancy, the sun, affection, disquietude, grief, jealousy, misery, cares*

marigold, African .... *vulgar-minded*

marigold, French .... *jealousy*

+marigold with red flowers ... *the varying course of life*

+marjoram, sweet .... *blushes, mirth, consolation, joy, happiness, kindness, courtesy, distrust*

marsh mallow .... *beneficence*

+mint .... *warmth of feeling*

+mint, lemon .... *virtue, homeyness, cheerfulness*

+mint, pineapple .... *hospitality, welcome*

mock orange/philadelphus ... *brotherly love, counterfeit*

monkshood .... *chivalry, deceit, a deadly foe is near* morning-glory .... *the evanescent loveliness of life*

moss .... *maternal love, ennui*

+mountain laurel/kalmia .... *ambition*

+mugwort .... *travel, prevents tiredness, Be not weary, helps conception, comfort*

mushroom .... *suspicion*

mustard seed .... *faith*

+myrtle .... *love, marriage, married bliss, fidelity, passion, peace, home, joy*

+myrtle, crepe .... *eloquence*

N

narcissus .... *egotism, self-love, self-esteem*

nasturtium .... *patriotism*

nerine .... *a nymph*

nettle .... *cruelty, slander*

+nettle, dead .... *preferred*

+nigella/love-in-a-mist .... *perplexity, embarassment, Kiss me twice before I rise, independence, prosperity*

O

+oak .... *hospitality, strength, independence, prosperity, longevity, truth, durabililty, steadfastness, virtue*

oats .... *music*

obedient plant/physostegia ... *obedience*

olive .... *peace, reconciliation, studious pursuit*

+olive, Russian .... *bitterness*

olive, tea .... *reward of literary merit*

+orange .... *chastity, bridal festivities, marriage, happy outcome, generosity, fecundity*

+orchid .... *luxury, love, refinement, nobility, scholarship, a belle, beauty, numerous progeny, lust, I await your favors*

orchid, cattleya .... *mature charms, matronly grace, flamboyant*

orchid, cymbidium .... *magnificence, scholarship, luxury, love, beauty*

orchid, lady's slipper .... *capricious beauty, desirable*

orchid, moth/phalaenopsis ... *evening joy*

+orchid, peacock/
acidanthera .... *distinction*

P

+pansy .... *thoughts, loving thoughts, You occupy my thoughts*

+parsley .... *festivity, thanks, gratitude, useful knowledge, feasting*

+parsley and rue together ...... *at the very beginning*

pasqueflower .... *You have no claims*

passion flower .... *Christian faith, religious superstition*

pea .... *departure, happy marriage, profits in business, respect*

pea, everlasting .... *an appointed meeting, lasting pleasure*

+pea, sweet .... *departure, delicate pleasures, Meet me, Adieu!, par excellence, tender memory*

+peach .... *longevity, I am your captive!, feminine softness, traditional flower of Girls' Day in Japan, ruddy health*

+pear .... *benevolent justice, affection, health, hope, longevity, good government, wise administration*

+pennyroyal .... *flee away*

+peony .... *beauty, welcome, bashfulness, hands full of cash*

peppermint .... *warmth, cordiality*

+perilla .... *role reversal*

periwinkle/vinca .... *love, pleasures of memory*

periwinkle, red .... *early friendship*

periwinkle, white .... *pleasant recollections*

phlox .... *Our souls are united, proposal of love, sweet dreams*

pimpernell, scarlet .... *assignation, change, rendezvous*

pincushion flower/scabiosa .. *unfortunate attachment, widowhood, I have lost all*

+pine .... *loyalty, vigorous life, endurance, boldness, longevity, warm friendship, spiritual energy, mobility*

+pine cone .... *fertility, life, the testes*

+pinks/dianthus .... *lively and pure affection, fascination, sweetness, boldness, newlyweds, dignity, taste, talent*

pinks, cheddar .... *woman's love, aspiration*

pinks, China .... *aversion*

pinks, cottage .... *childish trifle*

pinks, double .... *You will always be lovely, My love will never die*

+pinks, single .... *pure love, aversion*

pinks, striped .... *refusal, talent*

+pinks, white .... *ingenuity, talent, departure, refusal, mobility*

+plane tree/sycamore .... *genius, curiosity, reserve*

+plantain .... *pilgrimage, well-trodden path*

+plumbago .... *antidote*

+plum .... *courage, happiness, hardiness, perseverance, marriage, longevity, fertility*

+plum, purple-leaf .... *duty through hardship*

+pokeweed .... *a jibe, poking fun*

polyanthus/primula .... *pride of riches*

polyanthus, crimson .... *the heart's mystery*

polyanthus, lilac .... *confidence*

pomegranate .... *royalty, mature elegance, posterity, foppishness, fertility, abundance*

poppy .... *forgetfulness, sleep, oblivion, evanescent pleasure*

poppy, corn .... *consolation, enthusiasm*

poppy, orange .... *vanity*

+poppy, red .... *forgetfulness*

poppy, scarlet .... *fantastic extravagance*

poppy, white .... *My bane, my antidote, sleep*

+poppy mallow .... *wine cups*

+primrose .... *early youth, gaiety, innocence, sorrow*

primrose, evening .... *Wait for me!, inconstancy*

+princess tree/paulonia .... *benevolence*

protea/frilled panties .... *risqué*

+pussy-toes .... *never-ceasing remembrance*

Q

+Queen Anne's lace .... *haven, protection, I'll return*

+queen of the prairie .... *farsighted outlook*

queen's rocket .... *fashionable, You are the queen of coquettes!*

quince .... *cheers my soul, temptation, triteness*

R

+ragweed .... *nuisance*

+ragwort .... *I am humble but proud!*

ranunculus .... *You are rich in attractions, I am dazzled by your charms*

+raspberry .... *remorse, fulfillment, gentle-heartedness*

reed .... *complaisance, music*

+reed, flowering .... *confidence in heaven*

rhododendron .... *danger*

rhubarb .... *advice, fidelity, brouhaha*

+rocket .... *rivalry, queen of coquettes*

rosa mundi .... *You are merry, variety*

+rose .... *love, beauty, congratulations, reward of virtue, May you be pleased and your sorrows mine!, grace, joy, You are gentle, friendship, silence, unity*

rose, cabbage .... *ambassador of love*

rose, champagne .... *effervescence, vitality, devotion*

rose, cherry-red .... *merriment, sweetness of character derived from good works*

rose, China .... *beauty always new*

rose, coral .... *I admire your accomplishments, good fortune, longevity, beauty*

rose, cream .... *richness, perfection, best qualities*

rose, damask .... *brilliant complexion, beauty always new*

rose, eglantine .... *poetry*

+rose, gilded .... *excess*

rose, gold .... *absolute achievement*

rose, green .... *freshness, health, liberty*

rose, guelder/viburnum .... *good news, jubilation, age, winter of age*

rose, Japanese/kerria .... *never too late to amend*

rose, lavender .... *rarity, dignity*

+rose, lenten/hellebore .... *cure for melancholy, remedy for madness*

rose, moss .... *love, voluptuousness*

rose, musk .... *capricious beauty*

rose, peach .... *immortality, Your qualities, like your charms, are unequalled*

rose, pink .... *grace, beauty*

rose, purple .... *sorrow*

+rose, red .... *I love you, passion, desire, beauty, victory, harmony, joy, charm, luck, pride, martyrdom*

rose, red and white .... *creative force, joy, unity*

rose, rose-colored .... *shyness, beauty, pride, love* rose, shell-pink .... *youth, good health, femininity*

+rose, thornless..................... *early attachment*

+rose, white .... *unity, silence, Keep my secret, I am worthy of you, love, respect, beauty*

rose, withered white .... *Death is preferable to dishonor!, transient impressions, I am in despair!*

rose, yellow........................... *friendship, highest mark of distinction, jealousy, unfaithful, forgive and forget, decrease of love on better acquaintance*

+rosebud............................... *Your ignorance of love is sweet!, beauty and youth*

rosebud, moss....................... *confession of love*

+rosebud, pink .... *grace, beauty, gentleness, a young girl, You are lovely!*

rosebud, red.......................... *innocent hope, young and beautiful*

+rosebud, white..................... *a heart untouched by love, too young to love, purity*

+rosemary .... *remembrance, Your presence revives me!, fidelity, devotion, wisdom, good luck in the new year, strengthens the memory*

+rue...................................... *grace, repentance, clear vision, virtue, disdain, beginning anew*

rue, goat's............................. *reason*

rushes................................... *docility*

S

safflower .... *marriage, welcome*

+sage..................................... *domestic virtue, wisdom, skill, esteem, mitigates grief*

+sage, Jerusalem/phlomis ..... *pride of ownership, earthly delights*

sage, Mexican or velvet .... *eloquence, spectacular*

sage, pineapple...................... *hospitality, esteem, virtue*

+sage, purple-leaf .... *gratitude*

Saint-John's-wort/
hypericum............................. *You are a prophet, protection, superstition*

+salvia, blue .... *wisdom, I think of you!*

salvia, red.............................. *energy, forever thine*

satin flower .... *sincerity*

savory.................................... *mental powers*

+sedum/stonecrop .... *tranquility, welcome-home-husband-however-drunk-ye-be*

+sensitive plant/mimosa........ *sensibility, bashful modesty, Be careful, Do not hurt me!*

shamrock .... *luck, light-heartedness, Ireland*

slime fungus.......................... *opposition, resistance*

+snapdragon......................... *No!, presumption, You are dazzling, but dangerous!*

snowdrop/galanthus .... *consolation*

snowflake/leucojum.............. *purity, herald of spring*

soapwort .... *cleanliness*

+sorrel .... *parental affection, joy*

+sorrel, wood........................ *ill-timed wit, maternal love*

southernwood .... *jest, bantering*

spearmint .... *warmth of sentiment* speedwell/veronica .... *female fidelity*

spiderwort/tradescantia .... *esteem but not love, transient happiness*

+spirea .... *victory, conceit*

+spirea, blue/caryopteris .... *helpfulness*

spurge/euphorbia .... *welcome*

+spruce .... *farewell, hope in adversity, immortality*

starflower, spring/ipheion ..... *hope, vigilance*

+statice .... *never-ceasing remembrance, gratitude, dauntlessness*

statice, sea .... *sympathy, remembrance*

stephanotis/floradora .... *wedding, Will you accompany me to the East?*

+stock .... *promptness, lasting beauty*

+stonecrop/sedum .... *tranquility, welcome-home-husband-however-drunk-ye-be*

strawberry .... *perfect goodness, You are delicious, foresight, future promise*

+strawberry begonia .... *cleverness*

+strawflower .... *never-ceasing remembrance*

+sumac .... *resoluteness, intellectual excellence*

sunflower/helianthus .... *loyalty, adoration, haughtiness*

sweet flag .... *fitness*

+sweet pea .... *departure, delicate pleasures, Meet me*

sweet shrub .... *compassion, benevolence*

sweet sultan .... *felicity*

+sweet William .... *childhood, memory, gallantry, finesse, dexterity*

T

+tansy .... *stays miscarriages, I declare against you!*

+thistle .... *austerity, independence, grief*

+thistle, Scots .... *retaliation, vengeance, Never forget, Scotland*

thrift/armeria .... *sympathy, thrift*

throatwort/trachelium .... *neglected beauty*

+thyme .... *activity, bravery, courage, strength, manger herb*

+tiger flower .... *For once may pride befriend me!*

traveler's joy .... *safety*

+trefoil .... *providence*

truffle .... *surprise*

+tuberose .... *dangerous love, voluptuousness*

+tulip .... *fame, charity, the perfect lover, consuming love, happy years, memory*

tulip, pink .... *love, imagination, dreaminess*

+tulip, red .... *declaration of ardent love*

+tulip, variegated .... *beautiful eyes*

tulip, white .... *lost love*

tulip, yellow .... *hopeless love*

+tulip poplar .... *fame, retirement, rural happiness, among the noblest*

turtlehead/chelone .... *pleasure without alloy*

V

+valerian .... *accomodating disposition, drunk and blowsy*

+verbena .... *faithfulness, marriage, fertility*

+verbena, lemon .... *responsibility, attractive to the opposite sex*

verbena, pink .... *family union*

verbena, scarlet .... *sensibility, Unite against evil*

verbena, white .... *Pray for me, pure and guileless*

+vervain .... *good fortune, wishes granted*

violet .... *modesty, faithfulness, humility, simplicity, I return your love!*

violet, blue .... *faithfulness, love, modesty, loyalty*

violet, Parma .... *Let me love you!*

violet, purple........................ *You occupy my thoughts*

violet, sweet .... *sweetness, modesty*

violet, white .... *candor, spotless innocence, purity of sentiment*

violet, yellow .... *rural happiness*

virgin's-bower/clematis .... *filial love*

Virginia creeper .... *I cling to you both in sunshine and in shade*

W

+wallflower........................... *lasting beauty, she is fair, fidelity in adversity*

+walnut .... *intellect, strength of mind, strategem*

+weigela.............................. *Accept a faithful heart*

wheat .... *friendliness, prosperity, riches, worldly goods*

+willow .... *freedom, serenity, friendship, patience, forsaken*

+willow, pussy...................... *friendship, recovery from illness*

windflower/anemone............ *expectation, anticipation*

wisteria................................ *Welcome fair stranger, I cling to thee, helpless and delicate, daughter's sweetness*

+woodruff, sweet.................. *eternal life and rejoicing, cordiality, athletic victory*

+wormwood .... *affection, absence, bitterness, protection for travelers*

Y

+yarrow................................ *war, cure for heartache, health, sorrow, heals wounds, cure, dispels melancholy*

+yew .... *sorrow, penitence, immutability, perseverance*

Z

+zinnia .... *thoughts of absent friends*

GLOSSARY

Index of
Sentiments

A

abandon .... *grape*

abandonment .... *anemone, Japanese anemone*

absence .... *wormwood*

absolute achievement .... *gold rose*

accept a faithful heart .... *weigela*

acceptance .... *lilac*

accomodating disposition ..... *valerian*

accomplishment .... *laurel*

achievement in the Arts .... *laurel*

activity .... *thyme*

Adieu .... *sweet pea, pea*

administration, wise .... *pear*

admiration .... *carnation, especially red or yellow, heather*

adoration .... *sunflower*

adversity .... *wallflower*

advice .... *rhubarb*

affection .... *marigold, pear, wormwood*

affection, conjugal .... *geranium*

affection, generous and devoted .... *honeysuckle*

affection, lively and pure ...... *pink carnation, pinks*

afterthought .... *aster*

age, winter of .... *guelder rose/viburnum*

aggressiveness .... *lavender cotton*

ambition .... *ivy, mountain laurel*

ambition, female .... *white hollyhock*

amiability .... *jasmine*

antidote .... *plumbago*

ardor .... *fleur-de-lis/iris*

artifice .... *clematis*

the Arts .... *acanthus*

aspiration .... *foxtail lily, cheddar pinks*

aspiring .... *bellflower*

assignation .... *scarlet pimpernell*

athletic victory .... *sweet woodruff*

attachment, ardent .... *lavender, larkspur*

attachment, early .... *thornless rose*

attractive .... *foamflower, sea holly*

attractive to the opposite sex .... *lemon verbena*

austerity .... *thistle*

availability .... *wild or hardy geranium*

aversion .... *China or single pinks*

B

baby, newborn .... *English daisy*

baby's hands .... *Japanese maple*

bantering .... *southernwood*

bashfulness .... *peony*

bashful modesty .... *sensitive plant*

Be careful, do not hurt me! .... *sensitive plant*

Be not weary .... *mugwort*

beautiful eyes .... *variegated tulip*

beautiful, long .... *begonia*

beauty .... *camellia, pink carnation, cinnamon, daylily, delphinium, lilac, maple, orchid, especially cymbidium, peony, roses of all colors, pink rosebud*

beauty, capricious .... *lady's slipper orchid, musk rose*

beauty, lasting/unfading .... *carnation, wallflower, stock*

beauty, magnificent .... *calla lily*

beauty, neglected .... *throatwort*

beauty always new .... *China rose, damask rose*

beauty and youth .... *rosebud*

beauty in retirement .... *aster*

beauty, splendid .... *amaryllis*

beer .... *hops*

beginning anew .... *rue*

beginning, at the very .... *parsley and rue together*

belief .... *garden anemone*

a belle .... *orchid*

beloved daughter.................. *cinquefoil*

beneficence........................... *marsh mallow*

benevolence .... *princess tree/paulo-nia, sweet shrub*

benevolent justice................ *pear*

best qualities .... *cream rose*

best wishes.......................... *basil*

betrothal.............................. *red carnation*

Beware, I am fanciful!........... *begonia*

beware of excess .... *saffron crocus*

birth..................................... *dittany*

bitterness.............................. *Russian olive, wormwood*

bluntness.............................. *borage*

blushes................................ *sweet marjoram*

boastfulness .... *hydrangea*

boldness............................... *pine, pinks*

bonds of love .... *carnation, honeysuckle*

bravery................................ *thyme*

bridal favor.......................... *ivy geranium*

bridal festivities.................... *orange*

brouhaha.............................. *rhubarb*

C

candor.................................. *white violet*

capability.............................. *coneflower*

cares.................................... *calendula/pot marigold*

carousing .... *grape*

challenge.............................. *coral bells*

change.................................. *scarlet pimpernell*

charity .... *tulip*

charm .... *rose, especially red*

charm, feminine.................... *gardenia*

chastity .... *orange blossom*

cheerfulness........................ *buttercup, chrysan-themum, especially yellow, English daisy, lemon mint*

cheerful, always.................... *coreopsis*

cheers my soul .... *quince*

cheers the heart .... *ajuga/bugle*

childhood............................. *sweet William, geranium*

childishness .... *buttercup*

chivalry .... *flowering cherry, daf-fodil, monkshood*

Christian faith...................... *passion flower*

Christmas joy....................... *holly berries*

cleanliness........................... *soapwort*

cleansing .... *hyssop*

clear vision.......................... *rue*

cleverness .... *strawberry begonia*

coldness .... *chaste bush*

comfort................................. *chamomile, gerani-um, especially scent-ed, red, and scarlet, mugwort, pear, Queen Anne's lace*

comforting .... *ginger*

compassion........................... *bee balm, elderberry, sweet shrub*

complaisance .... *reed*

complexion, brilliant .... *damask rose*

conceit................................. *spirea*

conception aid .... *mugwort*

confession of love................. *moss rosebud*

confidence .... *lilac polyanthus*

confidence in heaven .... *flowering reed*

congratulations .... *rose*

conjugal affection .... *geranium*

conjugal love......................... *linden*

consolation .... *scarlet geranium, sweet marjoram, corn poppy, snowdrop*

constancy............................. *bellflower, wild or hardy geranium, ivy, calendula/pot marigold*

contentment......................... *camellia*

conviviality........................... *cone*

coquetry .... *yellow lily*

coquette .... *daylily*

cordiality .... *sweet woodruff*

counterfeit........................... *mock orange/philadelphus* courage .... *borage, plum, thyme, garlic chives, garlic*

courtesy................................... *sweet marjoram*

creative force .... *red and white rose*

creativity................................ *oregano*

cruelty .... *nettle*

cure .... *yarrow*

cure for heartache................. *yarrow*

cure for melancholy.............. *lenten rose/hellebore*

D

dainty pleasures.................... *coral bells*

danger .... *rhododendron*

dangerous love .... *tuberose*

dangerous pride.................... *blackberry*

daughter, beloved................. *cinquefoil*

daughter's sweetness............ *wisteria*

dauntlessness......................... *statice*

dazzling but dangerous .... *snapdragon*

a deadly foe is near............... *monkshood*

Death is preferable
to dishonor!........................... *withered white rose*

deceit...................................... *geranium, monkshood*

decision.................................. *foxglove*

declaration of love .... *tulip, especially red*

decrease of love
on better acquaintance .... *yellow rose*

delay....................................... *hardy ageratum*

delicacy .... *cornflower/bachelor's -button, dusty-miller, lily-of-the-valley*

delicate pleasures .... *sweet pea*

departure .... *white pinks, sweet pea, pea*

desertion .... *columbine*

desire...................................... *red rose*

devoted affection................... *honeysuckle*

devotion.................................. *lavender, hosta, hydrangea, champagne rose, rosemary*

dexterity .... *sweet William*

diffidence .... *cyclamen*

dignity .... *Silver King artemisia, dahlia, pinks, lavender rose*

directness .... *borage*

discretion .... *maidenhair fern, lemon blossom*

disdain.................................... *yellow carnation, rue*

dispels melancholy .... *yarrow*

disquietude .... *marigold*

distinction .... *cardinal flower, acidanthera/ peacock orchid*

distinction, highest mark of ... *yellow rose*

distrust.................................... *cyclamen, lavender*

Do not abuse.......................... *saffron crocus*

Do not forget me!.................. *forget-me-not*

docility .... *rushes*

domestic happiness .... *grape, holly*

domestic virtue .... *sage*

dreaminess.............................. *pink tulip*

dreams .... *sweet phlox*

drunk and blowsy.................. *valerian*

durability................................ *oak*

duty through hardship.......... *purple-leaf plum*

E

early attachment .... *thornless rose*

early friendship..................... *red periwinkle*

early youth .... *primrose*

earthly delights .... *Jerusalem sage*

education, good..................... *cherry, clover*

effervescence .... *champagne rose*

egotism.................................... *narcissus*

elegance.................................. *bleeding heart, Carolina jasmine, locust, maple*

eloquence .... *crepe myrtle, iris, Mexican or velvet sage*

embarrassment .... *nigella*

encouragement...................... *galax, goldenrod*

endurance .... *pine*

endurance in love .... *calendula/*
pot marigold
energy .... *red salvia*
energy in adversity .... *chamomile*
ennui .... *moss*
enthusiasm .... *Monte Cristo aster,*
bouvardia,
corn poppy
envy .... *wild or hardy*
geranium
esteem .... *sage, especially*
pineapple
esteem but not love .... *spiderwort*
eternal life .... *sweet woodruff*
the evanescent
loveliness of life .... *morning glory*
evening joy .... *moth orchid*
evil prevented .... *lavender cotton*
excellence .... *camellia*
excess .... *gilded rose*
expectation .... *anemone*
expected meeting .... *nutmeg-scented*
geranium
eyes, beautiful .... *variegated tulip*

F

faith .... *garden anemone,*
mustard seed
faithfulness .... *dogwood, verbena,*
violet, especially blue
falsehood .... *yellow lily*
fame .... *tulip poplar, tulip*
fame speaks him great
and good .... *apple*
family union .... *pink verbena*
fantastic extravagance .... *scarlet poppy*
farewell .... *spruce*
farsighted outlook .... *queen-of-the-prairie*
fascination .... *carnation, especially*
red or yellow, fern,
pinks
fashionable .... *queen's rocket*
fastidiousness .... *sensitive plant*

feasting .... *parsley*
fecundity .... *fig, orange*
felicity .... *bachelor's-button/*
cornflower, dusty-
miller, impatiens/
balsam, sweet sultan
female ambition .... *white hollyhock*
female fidelity .... *speedwell/veronica*
feminine charm .... *gardenia*
feminine modesty .... *calla lily*
feminine softness .... *peach*
femininity .... *shell-pink rose*
fertility .... *pine cone, plum,*
verbena
fertility and abundance .... *pomegranate*
festivity .... *parsley, baby's breath*
fickleness .... *pink larkspur*
fidelity .... *bleeding heart, ivy,*
myrtle, rhubarb,
rosemary
fidelity, female .... *speedwell/veronica*
fidelity in adversity .... *wallflower*
fidelity in love .... *lemon*
finesse .... *sweet William*
first emotions of love .... *purple lilac*
first love .... *white azalea*
fitness .... *sweet flag*
flamboyant .... *cattleya orchid*
flame .... *fleur-de-lis/iris*
flee away .... *pennyroyal*
the fleeting quality of life .... *grass*
flirt .... *daylily, feverfew*
folly .... *columbine,*
geranium, especially
scarlet
foolishness .... *pomegranate*
foppishness .... *pomegranate*
For once may pride
befriend me! .... *tiger flower*
force .... *fennel*
foresight .... *holly, strawberry*
forever thine .... *red salvia*
forgetfulness .... *opium poppy*
forgive and forget .... *yellow rose*

forgiveness............................ *creeping Jennie, gooseneck loosestrife*

forsaken .... *willow*

freedom................................. *willow*

freshness .... *green rose*

friendliness............................ *wheat*

friendship .... *galax, gerbera daisy, ivy, Peruvian lily/ alstromeria, pine, pussy willow, rose, especially yellow, willow*

friendship, early.................... *red periwinkle*

friendship, warm................... *pine*

fruitfulness .... *hollyhock, lily*

fulfillment............................. *raspberry*

fun.. *lemon balm*

future promise .... *buds, strawberry*

G

gaiety................................... *primrose, yellow lily, baby's breath*

gallantry .... *sweet William*

games.................................... *hyacinth*

generosity .... *gladiolus, globeflower, orange*

genius................................... *plane tree*

gentle-heartedness................ *raspberry*

gentleness .... *lamb's-ears, pink rosebud*

gift of Mother Earth.............. *corn*

gifts of the Holy Spirit .... *columbine*

Girls' Day flower (Japan)....... *peach*

gladness .... *sweet cicely*

gladness, youthful................. *crocus*

glory..................................... *laurel*

good fortune .... *goldenrod, coral rose, vervain*

good luck .... *bayberry, clover, gar-lic, white heather*

good luck in the new year ..... *rosemary*

good nature........................... *forsythia*

good news .... *guelder rose*

good taste.............................. *single dahlia*

good will .... *holly*

government, good .... *pear*

grace..................................... *Carolina jasmine, rose, especially pink, rue, pink rosebud*

grace, airy............................. *asparagus fern*

graceful .... *sea holly*

gracefulness .... *daffodil, white geranium*

gratitude .... *bellflower, dahlia, globeflower/trollius, parsley, purple-leaf sage, statice*

gratitude to parents............... *white dahlia*

great joy and delight .... *caladium*

grief...................................... *calendula/pot marigold, thistle*

to grow thin .... *fennel*

H

hands full of cash .... *peony*

happiness............................... *lavender, sweet marjoram, plum*

happy outcome...................... *orange*

happy years........................... *tulip*

hard work .... *coral bells, clover*

hardiness............................... *plum*

harmony................................ *red rose*

hatred.................................... *basil*

haughtiness............................ *amaryllis, double larkspur, sunflower*

Have pity on my passion! ...... *jonquil*

haven .... *Queen Anne's lace*

healing .... *lemon balm*

healing properties.................. *bachelor's-button, bluebottle/cornflower*

heals wounds......................... *yarrow*

health .... *bachelor's-button, geranium, especially red, calendula/ pot marigold, pear, green rose, yarrow*

150

I

innocence .... *daisy, English daisy, freesia, primrose*
innocence, spotless .... *white violet*
innocence, youthful.............. *white lilac*
innocent hope........................ *red rosebud*
insincerity............................ *cherry, foxglove*
inspiration .... *angelica*
instability.............................. *dahlia*
instruction .... *bayberry*
intellect .... *walnut*
intellectual excellence .... *sumac*
intoxication............................ *grape*
Ireland.................................. *shamrock*
irresistible............................. *dill*

J

jealousy .... *marigold, especially French, yellow rose*
jest.. *southernwood*
Jesus' manger herb .... *bedstraw, thyme*
a jibe..................................... *pokeweed*
joviality................................. *chrysanthemum*
joy .... *salad burnet, chrysanthemum, cal-endula/pot marigold, sweet marjoram, myrtle, oregano, rose, especially red or red and white, sorrel*
joys to come .... *wood sorrel*
jubilation .... *guelder rose/ viburnum*
justice .... *black-eyed Susan*
justice, benevolent................. *pear*
Justice shall be done you .... *coltsfoot*

K

Keep my secret .... *white rose*
keys.. *maple*
kindliness............................... *blue hyacinth*

kindness................................. *elderberry, sweet marjoram*
Kiss me twice before I rise..... *nigella*

L

lasting beauty........................ *stock*
lasting pleasure .... *everlasting pea*
liberty.................................... *green rose*
life .... *cone, pine cone*
life, long .... *chrysanthemum, euonymous*
light-heartedness .... *shamrock*
little boy flower..................... *anthurium/ flamingo flower*
living for love........................ *white carnation*
longevity .... *fig, peach, pine, plum, oak, pear, coral rose*
love .... *azalea, cinnamon, lemon balm, lilac, myrtle, orchid, peri-winkle, pinks, rose, especially red, rose-colored, or white, pink tulip, blue violet*
love, ambassador of.............. *cabbage rose*
love, ardent .... *impatiens/balsam, red tulip*
love, ardent and pure .... *carnation*
love, bonds of .... *carnation, honeysuckle*
love, brotherly .... *mock orange*
love, confession of................ *moss rosebud*
love, conjugal........................ *linden*
love, consuming .... *tulip*
love, dangerous .... *tuberose*
love, deep and pure............... *red carnation*
love, filial .... *virgin's-bower/ clematis*
love, first .... *white azalea*
love, first emotions of .... *purple lilac*
love, hopeless .... *yellow tulip*
love, living for....................... *white carnation*

N

newborn baby...................... *English daisy*

needing protection .... *gerbera daisy*

Never forget .... *Scots thistle*

never too late to amend........ *Japanese rose/kerria*

newlyweds........................... *pinks*

No!...................................... *snapdragon*

nobililty .... *flowering cherry,
orchid*

noblest, among the .... *tulip poplar*

nuisance.............................. *ragweed*

a nymph .... *nerine*

O

obedience .... *obedient plant*

oblivion............................... *poppy*

opposition............................ *slime fungus*

optimism .... *chrysanthemum*

Our souls are united .... *phlox*

P

panache .... *calla lily*

par excellence...................... *sweet pea*

parental affection................. *sorrel*

participation......................... *double dahlia*

passion................................ *red or laced carnation, myrtle, red rose*

path, well-trodden .... *plantain*

patience .... *allium/flowering
onion, chamomile,
oxeye daisy, dock,
willow*

patriotism .... *nasturtium*

peace................................... *gardenia, myrtle,
olive*

penitence .... *yew*

perfect goodness .... *strawberry*

the perfect lover................... *tulip*

perfection............................. *rose, especially cream*

perpetual concord .... *apple*

perplexity............................. *nigella*

perseverence........................ *magnolia, plum, yew*

personal achievement .... *laurel*

pilgrimage .... *plantain*

plant physician..................... *chamomile*

play .... *hyacinth*

pleasant............................... *ginger*

pleasantries .... *Peruvian lily/
alstromeria*

pleasure, lasting................... *everlasting pea*

pleasure without alloy .... *turtlehead*

pleasures, wordly .... *astilbe*

pleasures of hope .... *crocus*

pleasures of memory .... *periwinkle*

plenty .... *grape*

pliancy, strength through ...... *bamboo*

poetry.................................. *eglantine rose*

poking fun .... *pokeweed*

pomp................................... *dahlia*

popular oracle...................... *English daisy*

popularity .... *kalanchoe*

popular, highly .... *begonia*

posterity .... *pomegranate*

power.................................. *Silver King artemisia,
oak*

pray for me........................... *white verbena*

prayer.................................. *blueberry*

precaution............................ *goldenrod*

preference............................ *geranium, especially
scented, apple*

preferred .... *dead nettle*

present preference................ *apple-scented
geranium*

presumption .... *snapdragon*

pride.................................... *amaryllis, tiger lily,
rose-colored or red
rose, pink carnation*

pride, dangerous................... *blackberry*

pride of
newly-acquired fortune .... *auricula/primula*

pride of ownership .... *Jerusalem sage*

pride of riches...................... *polyanthus/primula*

profits in business................ *pea*

progeny, numerous .... *orchid*

promise .... *iris*

promise of
good things to come .... *buds*

promptness .... *stock*

proposal of love .... *phlox*

prosperity .... *grape, nigella, oak, wheat*

protection .... *blueberry, garlic, garlic chives, red geranium, juniper, Queen Anne's lace, Saint-John's-wort*

protection for travelers .... *wormwood*

protection from danger.......... *heather*

providence .... *trefoil*

pure and guileless .... *white verbena*

pure heart .... *baby's breath*

pure love of a virgin .... *cosmos*

purity .... *gardenia, white lilac, lily, lily-of-the-valley, white rosebud, snowflake*

purity of sentiment .... *white violet*

pursuit .... *lavender cotton*

Q

Queen of coquettes .... *rocket*

R

rarity .... *lavender rose*

rashness .... *butterfly bush*

recall...................................... *silver-leaf geranium*

reckless .... *mandevilla*

recollections, pleasant .... *white periwinkle*

reconciliation .... *olive*

recovery from illness .... *pussy willow*

refinement.............................. *gardenia, orchid*

refusal .... *Japanese anemone, striped carnation, striped or white pinks*

regard .... *daffodil*

rejected suitor .... *ice plant*

rejection .... *yellow carnation*

rejoice and
comfort the heart .... *sweet cicely*

rejoicing .... *sweet woodruff*

rejuvenation .... *lemon balm*

relief .... *lemon balm*

religious superstition .... *passion flower*

remedy for madness .... *lenten rose*

remembrance .... *forget-me-not, hydrangea, calendula/pot marigold, rosemary, statice, sea statice*

remembrance,
never-ceasing........................ *pussy-toes, statice, strawflower*

remorse .... *bramble, red or black raspberry*

rendezvous .... *chickweed, scarlet pimpernell*

repentance .... *rue*

reserve................................... *maple*

resistance .... *slime fungus*

resoluteness .... *sumac*

resolved to win .... *columbine*

respect................................... *daffodil, pea, white rose*

responsibility .... *lemon verbena*

rest.. *hops*

resurrection........................... *lily*

retaliation .... *Scots thistle*

retirement............................... *tulip poplar*

return of a friend is desired ... *delphinium, balloon flower/platycodon, bellflower/campanu-la together, bellfower*

return of happiness................ *lily-of-the-valley*

reward of literary merit.......... *tea olive*

reward of merit .... *laurel*

reward of virtue .... *rose*

rich in charms .... *buttercup*

riches...................................... *corn, wheat*

richness .... *cream rose*

righteousness .... *gentian*

risqué .... *protea*

rivalry .... *rocket*

role reversal .... *perilla*

romance .... *azalea*

royalty .... *pomegranate*

rural happiness .... *tulip poplar,*
yellow violet

S

sadness .... *dead leaves,*
gerbera daisy

safe .... *ginger*

safety .... *broom, traveler's joy*

scholarship .... *coral bells, orchid,*
especially cymbidium

Scotland .... *Scots thistle*

self-esteem .... *narcissus*

self-love .... *narcissus*

sensibility .... *sensitive plant*

sentimental recollections .... *aster, Silver King*
artemisia

separation .... *Carolina jasmine*

serenity .... *willow*

sharpens wit and
understanding .... *lemon balm*

showy .... *lisianthus*

shyness .... *peony,*
rose-colored rose

silence .... *rose, especially white*

silliness .... *cockscomb*

silver moonlight .... *Silver King artemisia*

simplicity .... *daisy, English daisy,*
violet

sincerity .... *fern, satin flower,*
anemone, sweet
cicely, honesty

skill .... *purple coneflower*

sleekness .... *glossy abelia*

sleep .... *hops, poppy,*
especially white

social intercourse .... *lemon balm*

softness .... *lamb's-ears*

softness, feminine .... *peach*

solitude .... *globeflower*

soothes the tremblings
and passions of the heart .... *lavender*

soothing .... *dill*

sorrow .... *primrose, purple rose,*
yarrow, yew

speak your mind .... *borage*

spectacular .... *Mexican sage*

spiritual energy .... *pine*

splendor .... *cardinal flower,*
Turk's-cap lily

sport .... *hyacinth,*
especially blue

spring, herald of .... *snowflake/leucojum*

steadfastness .... *oak, bamboo*

stoicism .... *box*

stratagem .... *walnut*

strength .... *fennel, garlic, lovage,*
oak, thyme

strength of character .... *gladiolus*

strength of mind .... *walnut*

strength through pliancy .... *bamboo*

strengthens the memory .... *rosemary*

studious pursuit .... *olive*

stupidity .... *geranium,*
especially scarlet

submission .... *grass*

success .... *laurel, lavender*

the sun .... *calendula/*
pot marigold

superstition .... *Saint-John's-wort*

support .... *lamb's-ears*

surprise .... *truffle, lamb's-ears*

suspicion .... *mushroom*

sweet dreams .... *phlox*

sweet virtues .... *bee balm*

sweetness .... *delphinium, lilac,*
especially white,
magnolia, pinks,
sweet violet

sweetness of character
derived from good works ...... *cherry,*
cherry-red rose

sympathy.............................. *lemon balm,*
sea statice, thrift

T

talent .... *oregano, pinks,*
especially white
taste .... *fuchsia, pinks*
temptation............................. *apple, quince*
tenacity.................................. *ivy*
the testes .... *pine cone*
thank you .... *daisy fleabane*
thanks.................................... *parsley*
thinness................................. *fennel*
thoughtlessness .... *mandevilla*
thoughts .... *pansy*
thoughts, happy..................... *heartsease/*
Johnny-jump-up
thoughts of absent friends ..... *zinnia*
thoughts of heaven .... *laurustinus/*
viburnum
thrift...................................... *thrift*
thriving.................................. *blackberry lily*
timidity .... *four o'clock, violet*
tiredness, prevents................ *mugwort*
a token of affection............... *oxeye daisy, laurusti-*
nus/viburnum
too young to love.................. *white rosebud*
tranquility.............................. *stonecrop/sedum*
transient happiness............... *spiderwort*
transient impressions............ *withered white rose*
transport of joy..................... *gardenia, jasmine*
travel .... *mugwort*
traveler's luck....................... *sea holly*
tree of life .... *arborvitae*
triteness................................ *quince*
the Trinity............................. *three-leaf clover*
trustfulness........................... *ivy*
trustworthiness .... *honesty*
truth...................................... *anemone, bittersweet,*
white chrysanthe-
mum, oak

U

unceasing remembrance .... *Silver King artemisia*
unchanged for eternity .... *clematis*
unchanging friendship .... *arborvitae*
unexpected meeting.............. *lemon-scented*
geranium
unfaithful.............................. *yellow rose*
unfortunate attachment .... *pincushion flower*
unity .... *white or red and*
white rose, allium/
flowering onion
uprightness .... *bamboo*
usefulness .... *grape hyacinth*

V

vanity .... *rocket*
variety .... *aster, rosa mundi*
the varying course of life .... *marigolds and red*
flowers together
vengeance.............................. *Scots thistle*
victory .... *red rose, spirea*
vigilance................................ *spring starflower*
vigorous life .... *pine*
virtue .... *lemon mint, oak, rue,*
sage, especially
pineapple
virtues, sweet .... *bee balm*
vision..................................... *rue*
vitality................................... *champagne rose*
voluptuousness...................... *cyclamen, tuberose,*
moss rose
voraciousness .... *lupine*
vulgar-minded .... *African marigold*

W

Wait for me!........................... *evening primrose*
wantoness .... *butterfly bush*
war .... *yarrow*

157

wards off evil .... *lavender cotton*
warm friendship..................... *pine*
warm-hearted .... *white cyclamen*
warming............................... *ginger*
warmth................................. *feverfew, peppermint*
warmth of feeling.................. *mints, all varieties*
warmth of sentiment............ *spearmint*
wealth .... *tiger lily*
wearisomeness,
helps against........................ *chamomile*
wedded love .... *ivy*
wedding................................ *stephanotis*
welcome .... *pineapple, pineapple mint, safflower, spurge*
Welcome, fair stranger........... *wisteria*
Welcome-home-husband-
however-drunk-ye-be............ *stonecrop*
welcome to new home .... *juniper*
well-being............................ *delphinium*
whimsy................................ *bells-of-Ireland*
widowhood .... *pincushion flower*
Will you accompany me
to the East? .... *stephanotis*
winecups............................... *poppy mallow*
wisdom .... *rosemary, sage, blue salvia*
wise administration............... *pear*
a wish................................... *foxglove*
wishes, best.......................... *basil*
wishes come true .... *dandelion seedhead, heather*
wishes granted...................... *gooseneck loosestrife, vervain*
wit, ill-timed......................... *wood sorrel*
the womb.............................. *fig*
womb plant........................... *creeping Jennie*
work, hard .... *coral bells, clover*
worldly goods....................... *wheat*
worldly pleasures .... *astilbe*
worth beyond beauty .... *sweet alyssum*
worthy of all praise............... *fennel*

Y

You are a prophet................. *Saint-John's-wort*
You are childish! .... *geranium*
You are dazzling
but dangerous...................... *snapdragon*
You are delicious! .... *strawberry*
You are lovely!...................... *pink rosebud*
You are merry .... *rosa mundi*
You are rich in attractions...... *ranunculus*
You are the queen of
coquettes.............................. *queen's rocket*
You are unjust!...................... *gentian*
You cannot deceive me .... *Japanese lily*
You have no claims .... *pasqueflower*
You light up my life! .... *feverfew*
You occupy my thoughts ...... *pansy, purple violet*
You pierce my heart .... *gladiolus*
You will always be lovely...... *double pinks*
a young girl .... *rosebud, especially pink*

Your ignorance of love
is sweet!................................. *rosebud*
Your image is engraven
on my heart! .... *euonymus*
Your looks freeze me!........... *ice plant*
Your presence revives me! .... *rosemary*
Your qualities, like your
charms, are unequalled! .... *peach rose*
Your smile bewitches me! ..... *scarlet geranium*
Your whims are
quite unbearable!.................. *bee balm*
Your wiles are irresistible! ..... *bergamot*
youth .... *lilac, rosebud*
youth, early .... *primrose*
youthful gladness.................. *crocus*
youthful innocence............... *white lilac*

Z

zeal....................................... *elderberry*
zest .... *lemon*

PICTURE CREDITS

Page 20: *Apollo and Daphne,* by Gian Lorenzo Bernini, 1622–24. Borghese Gallery, Rome. Canali Photobank, Capriolo (BS), Italy.

Page 22: "La Jonquille," from *La guirlande de Julie,* Paris, Didot Jeune, 1818. Courtesy of Hunt Institute for Botanical Documentation, Carnegie Mellon University, Pittsburgh.

Page 28: Aztec nobleman, by Ixtililxochitl, from *The De la Cruz-Badiano Aztec Herbal of 1552.* National Library of France, Paris.

Page 29: Composite photograph of Greek water jar, c. 450 B.C., private collection. Hirmer Verlag, Munich.

Page 30: Laurel wreath, photograph by Sheilah Scully, 1993.

Page 33: "Incunabulum of Courtly Taste," from *The Tacuinum of Paris,* c. 1380. National Library of France, Paris.

Page 35: Central panel from *Triptych of the Annunciation,* by Robert Campin, c. 1425–30. The Metropolitan Museum of Art, New York, The Cloisters Collection, 1956, (56.70).

Page 36: *The Infanta Maria Teresa,* by Diego Velázquez, c. 1660. The Prado, Madrid.

Page 38: *The Declaration of Love,* by J. F. de Troy, c. 1731. State Castle and Garden, Berlin.

Page 49: *Queen Victoria at the Opera,* engraving by C. E. Wagstaff, 1838, after a portrait by E. T. Paris from 1837. National Portrait Gallery, London.

Page 50: *Linen Polonaise,* engraving by Le Roy after Sebastien Le Clerc, 1776. Gallery of Fashion and French Costume, National Library of France, Office of Prints, Paris.